LIFE ISN'T ROCKET SCIENCE

by Jeff Canfield

Insight Publishing Group
Tulsa, Oklahoma

Life Isn't Rocket Science

Published by Insight Publishing Group
8801 S. Yale, Suite 410
Tulsa, Oklahoma 74137
918-493-1718

203 N. Seventh St.
St. Joseph, Illinois 61873
www.canfieldministries.org

Cover design by Banner Media

ISBN 1-930027-13-3
Printed in the United States of America

Contents

Dedication

To Courtney and Nathan: Don't be overwhelmed by life! Get to know our big God so well that everything you face in life will look small in comparison. And remember, Dad says, "Life isn't rocket science!"

Acknowledgments

My heartfelt thanks to:

My wife Lori for enduring many hours of *me on the computer,* and for your loving support!

Helen Canfield, Barbara Ryba, and Sue Baker for your *outstanding* editorial work, and for your support of this book!

Doug Jones for keeping me on track doctrinally.

John Meng for the photography.

Roger Bensyl for the web help.

Mom and Dad, what can I say? All those college English courses paid off!

Preface

Have you ever known a person who is very intelligent yet seems to have no common sense? You know the type: mathematician or chess master who cannot successfully operate a toaster; or the nuclear physicist who endangers people's lives while trying to parallel park his car.

The same is true in spiritual pursuits. There are many theologians who have devoted their lives to *higher criticism* of the Bible while overlooking the simplest truths of the Word of God which are able to save their souls.

While on the road to the *higher plane* (via Time Magazine) these same theologians convince *average* people that biblical truths are beyond their grasp as if there is some thick religious veil that cannot be pierced by common folk. This leaves many believing that they cannot assimilate biblical truths for themselves — so why even try?

Life (more specifically the Christian life) is not rocket science! Unless, of course, you're a rocket scientist. But even then only a small portion of your life (collectively speaking) is devoted to the extremely complicated, but fascinating, science of rockets.

The majority of life's situations are simply not that complicated. That's not to say that there's no need for sociologists, psychologists, and others who are trained in the science of human behavior. It is not my purpose in writing this book to demean those professions.

My purpose is to stimulate biblical patterns of thought which can assist individuals by giving them a true sense of biblical morality, ethics, vision, passion and purpose for their lives, thereupon launching them into a victorious life that is firmly established in God's Word. In other words — CUT THE PROBLEMS OFF AT THE PASS AND GO FOR THE GOLD!

In order to do this we must forge ahead determined that we are going to be doers of the word and not hearers only. James 1:22 says, *"But be doers of the word, and not hearers only,* ***deceiving yourselves.****"* It's one thing if I am deceived by someone else. But, if I deceive *myself*…! What can I say? That is the epitome of deception!

This book is for people who are lost on the road of life searching for answers; or for those who cannot find life's road hoping that there really are answers; or for those who are familiar with life's answers and simply need a kick in the seat of the pants. So as you begin to turn the pages of this book, be prepared to take a giant barbecue spatula, pry your posterior up off the couch, and become a doer of the Word.

Chapter 1

(Introduction)

Why Did the Chicken Cross the Road?

Q. Why did the chicken cross the road?

Answers:

Bill Gates:
I have just released the new Chicken 2010, which will both cross roads AND balance your checkbook, though when it divides 3 by 2 it gets 1.499999999.

Bill Clinton:
I don't recall.

Richard M. Nixon:
The chicken did not cross the road. I repeat, the chicken did not cross the road.

Saddam Hussein:
This was an unprovoked act of rebellion and we were quite justified in dropping 50 tons of nerve gas on it.

Dr. Seuss:
Did the chicken cross the road?
Did he cross it with a toad?
Yes! The chicken crossed the road,
but why it crossed it, I've not been told!

Ernest Hemmingway:
To die. In the rain.

Grandpa:
In my day, we didn't ask why the chicken crossed the road. Someone told us that the chicken had crossed the road, and that was good enough for us.

Colonel Sanders:
I missed one? [1]

As I recall, the answer to this children's joke is, "To get to the other side." I've used this parody to help illustrate how we can take life's simplest situations and overcomplicate them.

---

[1] *Why Did the Chicken Cross the Road?* Author unknown.

As human beings, we seem to enjoy tossing as much drama and intrigue as we can into life's situations. We can see this in our media-crazed culture by examining the most popular shows on television and the movies which play at our theaters. Hollywood can script an entire movie or TV drama around what amounts to a simple moral or ethical decision: for example, choices concerning adultery, premarital sex, abortion, drugs, and so on.

It's also sad to say that many people live their lives vicariously through television and movies. The danger in this scenario is that so often the entertainment industry conveys a false *fantasy world view* after which a person may try to pattern his life.

As a result, this person might be disappointed with his own life because it doesn't mimic what he's viewed on the big screen. Before long he becomes dissatisfied with his seemingly dull existence and tries to accentuate his life with material possessions or affairs of one sort or another. In which case, **morality, conscience, commitment, and faithfulness quickly become antiquated ideals**.

If we want to have purpose and direction in our lives, to live a life that's pleasing to God and has a profound impact on others, then we need to know what God's Word has to say about *everyday life issues* **and** put the Word of God into action in our lives. The truth is, life is not that complicated and ***neither is the Bible!***

Blow The Clouds Away

A cartoon by Mark Pie, which appeared in *New Wine* magazine, also helps illustrate how we can overcomplicate things. It showed a professor beginning a lecture to his class on "Communication" with these words:

"Communication is any modus operandi by or through which eventuates the reciprocal transposition of information between or among entities or groups via commonly understood systems of symbols, signs, or behavioral patterns of activity."

The answers to most real life questions are hardly mysterious and most of the time are right in front of our noses. It's understood that sometimes our lives do include difficult situations that are outside the realm of our control. However, the problems that I am referring to are *moral, ethical, and spiritual decisions* that affect our everyday lives. I'm talking about ordinary decisions that *are* within the realm of our control, and can easily be handled by making godly choices. I believe that much of the complexity of these *everyday situations* is of our own making.

We've all known someone who has clouded an issue with misguided, overcomplicated conclusions. Then as the truth unfolds, it becomes clear that in their *conscience* they understood what was morally and ethically correct. The facts show the issue was intentionally obscured by spinning a web of misinformation and deceit.

Of course, during the *crisis* everyone understood because it was so stressful, and the issue was *far too perplexing* for the average person to investigate. At that point, if that person is challenged concerning true motives, the challenger is accused of being too self-righteous and judgmental. Those types of accusations are meant to silence everybody close to the situation so that there's no accountability for wrongdoing.

Too often this resembles our efforts to understand and implement biblical truths. We claim that the scriptures are too difficult to understand. This provides us with an excuse to not make the slightest effort to understand the Bible or put into practice biblical principles. Unfortunately, our ignorance of the Word of God can also yield the wrong perception of who God is and what His will is for our lives.

As a result, when difficulties in life arise, many times we blame God or others for our problems. Even if it is gently explained to us that maybe our problems are of our *own* making, we denounce the person who is explaining this as being holier-than-thou. Those attitudes and excuses will not hold up with God!

Nine times out of ten it's not the answer to the *problem* that's difficult to ascertain. What's difficult is having the *intestinal fortitude* (or guts) to act upon what we know is the truth, regardless of personal consequences.

Let's blow the clouds away from complicated issues in our life by facing the facts and being totally honest before God and others. Being completely transparent before God, allowing Him to search our hearts, is undoubtedly the starting point of a successful Christian walk. Let's have the courage to live a life of integrity and honor. Proverbs 28:13 says, *"He who covers his sins will not prosper, but whoever* ***confesses and forsakes*** *them will have mercy."* **Honesty truly is the best policy.**

Get to the Heart of the Matter!

I love to read how Jesus dealt with difficult situations. One example is when the scribes and Pharisees brought a woman caught in adultery to Jesus. Jesus listened as they explained the situation. The true motive of the scribes and Pharisees was to entrap Jesus in a dilemma. (See John 8.)

Regardless, Jesus completely burst their bubble as He plunged directly into the heart of the matter. Jesus said, *"He who has no sin cast the first stone!"* **Boom! Over and done with!** I can picture the Pharisees sheepishly walking away while childishly thinking to themselves, "He spoiled all our fun!"

Then Jesus said to the woman, *"Woman, where are those accusers of yours? Has no one condemned you?"* It sounds as though Jesus loved the irony of the situation. Most importantly, Jesus told the woman, "Neither do I condemn you; go and sin no more." Too simple? I don't think so. Jesus knew how to cut right to the heart of a matter.

Albeit, 2000 years later, scholars and *higher critics* try to add intrigue to the story by speculating as to what Jesus was writing on the ground. Wouldn't it be interesting if Jesus was simply doodling and thinking to Himself, "Why don't these people get a life!"

I believe the woman caught in adultery realized and received the great mercy and forgiveness that had been given to her. Jesus not only forgave the woman, but afterward left her with a **definite command to act upon what she had received**. We **must** act upon the knowledge we receive! Faith must be accompanied by works, and works must be accompanied by faith — the two go hand-in-hand. (See James 2:17-18.)

In order for our faith in God to be beneficial in our lives, and the lives of others, we must acquire knowledge of God. We must also gain an understanding of how God's Word pertains to our *everyday lives* so we may put His Word into practice.

> *My people are destroyed for lack of knowledge.*
>
> *Hosea 4:6*

Wise people store up knowledge, but the mouth of the foolish is near destruction.
Proverbs 10:14

Second Peter 3:18 speaks of the knowledge we are to grow in, *"...but grow in the grace and knowledge* ***of our Lord and Savior Jesus Christ.****"* Romans 10:17 tells us how to gain a firm trust and reliance in the Word of God, ***"So then faith comes by hearing, and hearing by the Word of God."***

Some might say, "That's all well and good, but the Bible is *so hard* to understand." I know there are certain subjects in the Bible that because of their complex nature require a substantial amount of research in order to attain the proper scriptural interpretation. However, even when interpreting difficult passages we still must have a solid foundation concerning basic scriptural truths.

Consider this analogy a pastor once gave: "A science museum may have many fascinating and highly technical exhibits which, in and of themselves, are more complex than the structure which embodies them. However, if the building which houses these scientific exhibits has been constructed on a faulty foundation it would not be prudent to fill it with such a wealth of knowledge." Kids today would probably say it like this, "Dude! Don't put extremely — **(choose 1: gnarly, way cool, awesome)** — stuff in a cruddy ol' box!"

Once we understand basic biblical principles, we must implement those principles in our lives. If we do not include *action* with our faith we will not see results. Trust me when I say that no one cares how many Bible verses we can quote if we refuse to walk in godly character never putting into practice scriptural principles that will make us stand out amongst non-believers.

Why did the chicken cross the road? To get to the other side! This book is designed for those who desire to know about, *and implement*, scriptural truths concerning: **taking responsibility, work ethics, pursuing your dreams, gossip, making godly choices, and keeping up with the Joneses**. These are a *few* of life's issues that affect most of us on a daily basis.

So before we explore the really deep theological questions (i.e. Where did God come from? Did Adam and Eve have belly buttons? Can God make a rock so big He can't lift it?), let's examine some real life issues in **light of what the Bible says**.

GOD'S WORD IS WHAT BRINGS AN OTHERWISE COMPLICATED EXISTENCE INTO FOCUS.

Chapter 2

Get Your *But* Out of the Way

"It has been said that an excuse is a thin skin of falsehood stretched tightly over a bald-faced lie."

Now that we know *why* the chicken crossed the road, let's discuss what the Rhode Island Red does once he reaches the other side. Let's dive right in by talking about excuses. We've all heard the excuses haven't we? Or, maybe we've been guilty of making these excuses.

I'm talking about people making excuses concerning their past saying, "*But* I just can't live a godly life because of my past;" or people who refuse to take responsibility for their actions, making statements like, "*But* you don't understand, it's not my fault;" or people who say they believe in God, but reject His Word while making excuses for their lack of commitment by saying, "I was going to come to church last Sunday, *but…*" Many times these folks wind up feeling as if they are destined for failure.

When I was growing up there was a popular show named Hee Haw. One of Hee Haw's comedy sketches began with several old hillbillies lying around outside a log cabin singing:

> *"Gloom, despair, and agony on me. Deep dark depression, excessive misery. If it weren't for bad luck, I'd have no luck at all. Gloom, despair, and agony on me."*

Once again, we probably all know someone who has that type of outlook on life. They say, "I just can't get anywhere in life! Everyone is against me!" A person with that attitude is headed toward mediocrity or failure. We should have great compassion for these people! I feel as if God would like to cry out to them, **"IT DOESN'T HAVE TO BE THAT WAY!"**

Every now and then we come across a heart wrenching, tear jerking, awe-inspiring television story or magazine article of a person who has overcome tremendous obstacles in life. Most of us have seen or heard these types of stories.

For instance:

A tragic event causes an up and coming track star to lose his leg. He's fitted with a prosthetic leg and he struggles through months and months of physical therapy and rehabilitation. His first time back on the track his leg hurts so much he feels like giving up. The mental and physical strain is almost too much to bear. But he doesn't quit! He musters all the courage he has, and eventually he's running again.

Maybe we don't have the best education. Maybe we didn't have the privilege of having great parents. Maybe we didn't grow up in the best neighborhood. Maybe we have a physical handicap that prevents us from doing some of the things others can. Just as those people we see and read about conquer overwhelming odds and rise above their self pity and self doubt — **SO CAN WE!**

In 2 Peter 1:3-4 it tells us that *"**His divine power** has given to us all things that pertain to life and godliness, **through the knowledge of Him** who called us by glory and virtue, by which have been given to us exceedingly great and precious promises, that through these you may be partakers of the divine nature, having escaped the corruption that is in the world through lust."* God tells us that He has given us everything that pertains to life and godliness. Christians are not victims — we are overcomers through Christ! **We have no excuse!**

Leave Your Behind Where It Belongs!

We live in a society that is full to the brim with excuses. H. V. Adolt said, "We are all manufacturers in a way — making good, making trouble, or making excuses." Everyone has a reason for why they can't stay married; or why they can't stop drinking; or why they abuse their children; or why they can't hold a job; or why, why, why,
whine,
whine,
whine… "Well, you don't understand! It goes all the way back to my great-great-grandfather. He was an alcoholic and so *I'm an alcoholic*."

There are even some in the Christian community who aid excuse makers with *scriptural proof* that the *root* of their problems is hereditary. This makes people feel as though there's nothing that can be done, that they are victims of GENERATIONAL CURSES.

I have never understood how we can become **"a new creature in Christ**, old things passed away, and behold **ALL THINGS HAVE BEEN MADE NEW"** (2 Corinthians 5:17), yet still be subject to something our grandfather did or something our grandmother had.

Exodus 20:5 is a scripture some folks use to back up the idea of generational curses. They conveniently quote the second part of Exodus 20:5 which says, *"...visiting the iniquities of the fathers upon the children to the third and fourth generations."* In other words, "The way that I'm acting isn't my fault. This behavior was handed down to me as a result of the iniquity (sin) of my great-grandfather.

Exodus 20:5 *might* help prove their case except there is much more in that passage. In Appendix B, I spell out a few basic rules of Bible interpretation. (Feel free to peek.) One of those rules states that we must consider what the surrounding verses say. Doing that will help give us an overall picture of the context of the passage.

The context of Exodus 20:5 is the Ten Commandments. The Israelites had this rather uncanny ability to let their affections and worship gravitate toward other gods. The first commandment God gives them is that they shall have NO other gods before Him.

Let's take a look at the context of this portion of scripture:

Exodus 20:3-4 — *You shall have no other gods before Me. You shall not make for yourself a carved image — any likeness of anything that is in heaven above, or that is in the earth beneath, or that is in the water under the earth.* (This was obviously for the purpose of worshipping false gods — Yes, of course throw out your little Buddha because it's a false god, but I don't see the need to throw out your grandma's plaster hand-painted patriotic bald eagle she has on her mantle); v.5 — *You shall not bow down to them nor serve them. For I, the Lord your God, am a jealous God, visiting the iniquity of the fathers upon the children to the third and fourth generations (that's where many people stop, but God goes on) of those who hate Me,* v.6 — ***BUT SHOWING MERCY TO THOUSANDS, TO THOSE WHO LOVE ME AND KEEP MY COMMANDMENTS."***

> *Therefore we make it our aim, whether present or absent, to be well pleasing to Him.*
>
> *For we must all appear before the judgment seat of Christ,* ***that each*** *one may receive the things done in the body,* ***according to what he has done****, whether good or bad.*
>
> *Knowing, therefore, the terror of the Lord, we persuade men; but we are well known to God, and I also trust are well known in your conscience.*
>
> *2 Corinthians 5:9-11*

We are not subject to nor do we have to answer to God for something our parents or grandparents did. We each have to stand before the judgment seat of Christ and answer for what we do in this life. Romans 14:12 also tells us, ***"So then each of us shall give an account of himself to God."***

Furthermore, Ezekiel 18:19-20 says, *"Yet you say,* ***'Why should the son not bear the guilt of the father?'"*** *The question is asked, and God lays the answer out very clearly: "Because the son has done what is lawful and right, and has kept all My statutes and observed them, he shall surely live. The soul who sins shall die.* ***The son***

shall not bear the guilt of the father, nor the father bear the guilt of the son. The righteousness of the righteous shall be upon himself, and the wickedness of the wicked shall be upon himself."

It's true that before we accepted Jesus as our Savior we were extremely vulnerable to the wiles of the devil because we were not covered by the blood of Jesus. Even after we're born again we must submit ourselves to God, then resist the devil by not giving in to his temptations. (See James 4:7.) Nevertheless, generational curses, or going back and repenting for the sins of our ancestors, is not scriptural and has no part of our *Christian* life unless we allow it to. Question: Do we hate God? If we're Christians obviously our answer would be "No." Really, it's very simple — if we love God, His promise to us is **mercy**!

Let me reiterate that when we accept Jesus as our Savior, old things pass away and **all things** become new. When the Bible says, "All things have become new," I believe it means ALL THINGS!

Our past is taken care of through the shed blood of Jesus! We need to leave our past in the past and not let the devil, or anyone else, dig up our past and remind us of sins we committed before we were a Christian. We're new creatures in Christ Jesus! Remind the devil that all that old junk has been covered by the blood of Jesus! Jesus said, "Therefore if the Son makes you free, **you shall be free indeed.**" **SO BE FREE IN JESUS NAME!**

Our future lies *ahead* of us, **not behind us**! Remember, if we're constantly looking back at our past while trying to walk into the future, we will not only get off course but we may also hurt ourselves and others.

Respond To Responsibility!

We have to take responsibility for what we do, *or don't do*, in this life. Let me use overeating as an example. (That hits me right above the belt!) Instead of putting the time and effort into controlling our flesh, we would rather have a minister "lay hands" on us to be *delivered* from the "bondage" of gluttony. As a result, the phrase has been coined — "fast-food Christianity." It's like driving up to a fast-food drive-through, ordering something, then a minute later grabbing your meal and driving off. Very little effort involved. *Very little faith involved.* Hebrews 11:6 says, *"without faith it is* ***impossible*** *to please God."*

I do believe, however, that *bad traits* can be passed down from one generation to another. That stands to reason. I thank God I had Christian parents who raised my brothers and me in the nurture and admonition of the Lord! However, if my dad had been a drunken wife beater, and I grew up in that type of environment with that kind of example — guess what? Without the saving grace and the power of God in my life, I might have grown up, married, and become a drunken wife beater.

Still, those types of cycles can easily be broken in families. How? It's called salvation! Becoming a new creature in Christ — *old things* passing away, and **all things** becoming new.

C. I. Scofield gives this definition of salvation from the Greek and Hebrew: "The Hebrew and Greek words for salvation imply the ideas of deliverance, safety, preservation, healing, and soundness. Salvation is the great inclusive word of the gospel, gathering into itself all the redemptive acts and processes, including: justification, redemption, grace, propitiation, imputation, forgiveness, sanctification, and glorification." It sounds all-inclusive to me! **And, thank God that it is!**

> *But when the fullness of the time had come, God sent forth His Son, born of a woman, born under the law,*
>
> *To redeem those who were under the law, that we might receive the adoption as sons.*
>
> *And because you are sons, God has sent forth the Spirit of His Son into your hearts, crying out, "Abba, Father!"*
>
> ***Therefore you are no longer a slave but a son, and if a son, then an heir of God through Christ.***
>
> *Galatians 4:4-7*

When we are born again our human spirit is re-created *by the power of the Holy Spirit*, and we become a child of God. (See Galatians 3:26-29.) As we just saw in Galatians 4: 4-7 we come into fellowship with the Almighty God, **and He becomes our Father!** This free gift of salvation, which includes all the benefits of being a child of God, and eternal life after we die, is the greatest gift ever given to mankind!

This whole salvation thing might sound too easy to some. Becoming a Christian *is* a new *BEGINNING*, but keep in mind that it's just the beginning. After being born again **(which is a free gift)** the Bible talks about *renewing the mind.*

In chapters one through eleven of the book of Romans, Paul laid out God's great plan of salvation. Then, in light of God's great redemptive work Paul says in Romans 12: 1-2, "I urge you therefore, brethren, by the same mercies of God, that you present your bodies a living sacrifice, holy, acceptable to God, **which is your reasonable**

service. And do not be conformed to this world, *but be transformed by the renewing of your mind,* **that you may prove what is the good and acceptable and perfect will of God**."

What comes after the redemptive work of Christ? The apostle Paul explains that the act of presenting our bodies holy and acceptable to God is our *reasonable* service. In essence, the apostle Paul is saying, "My goodness, men, considering the great gift you've been given, presenting your bodies holy and acceptable to God is the only *reasonable thing* you can do in return!" When we present our bodies as a "living sacrifice" we are, in fact, giving honor to God by worshipping Him *with our very lives*.

With those thoughts in mind, once we're born again the Father sees us through Christ-colored glasses. We now have a "robe of righteousness" given to us as a *free gift* when we confess with our mouth that Jesus is Lord, and believe in our heart that God raised Him from the dead. (See Romans 10:9-10 and Isaiah 61:10.) But our mind, our will, and our emotions need a lot of work. (Thanks a lot, Jeff!) Don't worry, though — God is longsuffering.

Older, more mature Christians, need to take younger ones under their wing and help them not become discouraged! Like newborns in the natural, spiritual newborns may soil their pants once in a while. But, just like a good earthly father, God helps us clean up through the word and through the friendships of fellow Christians. I don't expect my six-year-old to be mature enough to go out and get a job so he can support himself. (Although my nine-year-old thinks she can!) That would be unfair of me! My six-year-old is not capable of supporting himself. Now, if my son was twenty years old and still expecting dad to wipe his bottom — we've got a problem!

God will allow us to grow in our faith giving us all the necessary tools we need **if** we will put ourselves in a position to receive them. That's what some Christians don't seem to comprehend. They think they can skip church all the time, get involved in worldly things, and still grow in their faith. Then when all hell breaks loose they blame God. They say, "Where did God go?" And God is saying, "Where did YOU go?" In reality it was their own lack of involvement in church (being taught the Word of God and worshipping God), and lack of Christian fellowship that produced their problems.

Once again, when we're born again our *human spirit* is renewed by the power of the Holy Spirit. However, our mind, our will, and our emotions are something **we** have to work on. In James 1:21-22, James (writing to Christians) says, *"Therefore lay aside all filthiness and overflow of wickedness, and receive with meekness the* ***implanted word****, which is able* ***to save your souls*** [mind, will, and emotions]. *But [here's an important key]* ***be doers of the word, and not hearers only, deceiving yourselves."***

Our mind, will, and emotions are changed through hearing the Word of God, receiving the Word of God (with patience and humility), *and* then putting what we've heard into practice in our lives. Why do we do this? Remember what Romans 12:1-2 said? Not only is it our *reasonable service*, but it also proves (shows the genuine authenticity of) God's good, acceptable, and perfect will.

The good news is that we have God's help to become the person He wants us to be. Hebrews 4:15-16 tells us, *"For we do not have a High Priest who cannot sympathize with our weaknesses, but was in all points tempted as we are, yet without sin.* ***Let us therefore come boldly to the throne of grace, that we may obtain mercy and find grace to help in time of need."***

Plus, we're not subject to the failures of our past! We are new creatures in Christ! We have a whole new frontier of possibilities available to us! And better yet, when we mess up — **He forgives us!** (See 1 John 1:9.)

When I say that we're not subject to the failures of our past, I'm talking about the spiritual realm. God sees us as a brand new person! Beware, however, if we embezzled $20,000 just before we were born again; people in the law enforcement community **will** hold us accountable — they're kind of funny that way. Point being, if we've made mistakes in *the natural realm* before we gave our life to the Lord — more than likely we will have to answer for them. WELL THEN, WHAT'S THE USE IN GETTING SAVED?

There are so many benefits to being born again! Let me review a few of the biggies — 1) No matter what happens to us in this life, we now have a clean past (spiritually), *and* eternal life with the Father after this life is over. 2) When we *"mess up"* we can repent to the Father, and in the name of Jesus, He will forgive us according to I John 1:9. And 3) Now that we're a child of God, *if* we will seek Him with our whole heart, He will help us *through* our trials (whether literal or figurative).

You see, God wants us to put all our excuses aside, look into His Word, and say to ourselves, "I want to be, **and I can be**, just like Jesus!" (See 1 Corinthians 11:1 and John 14:12.)

Fear God and Get Excited About Your Future!

The children in a prominent family decided to give their father a book of the family's history for a birthday present. They commissioned a professional biographer to do the work, carefully warning him of the family's "black sheep" problem: Uncle George had been executed in the electric chair for murder. The biographer assured the children, "I can handle that situation so that there will be no embarrassment. I'll merely say that Uncle George occupied a chair of applied electronics at an important government institution. He was attached to his position by the strongest of ties and his death came as a real shock." [2]

God can do even better! God doesn't have to whitewash our past. Allow me to say for the last time — when we're born again **"All things become new."** As I've already mentioned, if we make mistakes after we're born again, 1 John 1:9 tells us that, *"If we confess our sins, He is faithful and just to forgive us our sins and to cleanse us from all unrighteousness."*

Psalms 103:11-12 states, *"For as the heavens are high above the earth, so great is His mercy toward those who fear Him; As far as the east is from the west, so far has He removed our transgressions from us."* Keep in mind the scriptures say, **"...toward those who fear Him."** In other words, toward those who have a reverential fear and respect for the Almighty God!

When we truly have a revelation of the fact that we will have to stand before the judgment seat of Christ and answer for what we have done it changes the way we think, the way we talk, and the way we act. A true reverential fear and respect for the God who created the heavens and the earth, and who will judge all who have ever lived upon the earth, will season everything we do with meekness, humility, and obedience to the Word of God!

---

[2] Source unknown.

The fear of the Lord is the beginning of wisdom.

Proverbs 9:10

Blessed is every one who fears the Lord, who walks in His ways.

When you eat the labor of your hands, you shall be happy, and it shall be well with you.

Your wife shall be like a fruitful vine in the very heart of your house, your children like olive plants all around your table.

Behold, thus shall the man be blessed who fears the Lord.

Psalms 128:1-4

You need to get past your past! Take responsibility for your actions! Don't give in to your flesh! If you fear God and obey His Word, your conscience will be as white as snow and your future will be bright as the sun at the equator!

DON'T ALLOW EXCUSES TO ROB YOU OF GOD'S BLESSINGS!

Chapter 3

Go to the Ant, You Sluggard!

"There are two kinds of men who never amount to very much," Cyrus H. K. Curtis remarked to his associate, Edward Bok.

"And what kinds are those?" inquired Bok.

"Those who cannot do what they are told," replied the famous publisher, "and those who can do nothing else."

Hi-ho, Hi-ho, it's off to work we go...

Since the beginning of time, God has given man chores to do. In the Garden of Eden, Adam was given the responsibility to tend the Garden. (See Genesis 2:15.) It obviously wasn't the type of work he would be compelled to do later. We know this because when man fell (sinned, disobeyed God) God told him that now he would till the ground and it would only produce *by the sweat of his brow*. (See Genesis 3:17-19.)

I've said, and I've heard others say, "**Man**, if Adam just wouldn't have sinned, we would still be in the Garden." Well, most of the time I'm an unbearable optimist, but come on! Imagine if Adam hadn't sinned and mankind (women included) were somehow able to keep all God's commands. Understand, of course, that the odds of that are impossible to calculate. Then some 6000 years, and countless generations later, it came down to us. Would *we* be able to go through life keeping all of God's commands and never giving in to the flesh? Maybe we should cut Adam a little slack, huh?

At any rate, 6000 plus years later we still have to put our hands to the plow. So let's talk about work ethics and why we must get up off our duffs and do something.

Work Isn't a Four-Letter Word!

The word "work" appears in the Bible 564 times! In 2 Thessalonians 3:10-11 it says, *"For even when we were with you, we commanded you this: If anyone will not work,* ***neither shall he eat****. For we hear that there are some who walk among you in a disorderly manner, not working at all, but are busybodies."*

What do people do when they refuse to work? Generally, people either become busybodies, or couch potatoes — lazyboys — bedbugs! When I talk about work ethics, I realize that there are many people who are not able to work due to disabilities. I'm referring to those who are able to work and simply choose not to.

The apostle Paul used some pretty strong language when talking about work ethics! Paul commanded them that if anyone "will not work, neither shall they eat." Many folks today would accuse Paul of being mean-spirited and out of touch. Proverbs 18:9 says, *"He who is slothful in his work is a brother to him who is a great destroyer."*

The rule in our house when I was growing up was this: If we went to college we could live at home for free, but if we didn't go to college we had to pay room and board. You say, "Man, you're kidding me! Room and board! You must have grown up in the 40s!" No, I graduated from high school in the early 80s. The message my parents were sending me was this: You better begin to do something with your life because you're not getting a free ride, and you're certainly not living at home forever! After I moved out they made my bedroom into a dining room! I think they were trying to send me a message.

Today we see too many young men living at home who are in their early 20s, not going to school, and not making any attempt to work. Dad (if he's around) needs to take Junior Sluggard aside and have a heart-to-heart chat. I'm talking about a loving, but stern, heart-to-heart talk where Dad's shoe leather is being firmly planted on Junior's back seat.

Adrian Rogers, former president of the Southern Baptist Convention, tells about the man who made his sons work in the cornfields while their peers spent the afternoon at the swimming hole. Someone scolded the father saying, "Why do you make those boys work so hard? You don't need all that corn."

The wise father replied, "Sir, I'm not raising corn. I'm raising young men."

My ears are burning as I hear folks say, "Man, Jeff, you're being so hard!" The fact is, if we treat a young man like a boy that's exactly what we'll have.

I see the proud look on my dad's face when his sons work hard and provide for their families. It not only pleases my earthly father, but also my heavenly Father. When you see an able-bodied young man in his early 20s hanging around the house not doing anything productive, you'll also find an unhappy mother and father. Proverbs 17:25 tells us, *"A foolish son is a grief to his father, and bitterness to her who bore him."*

When it comes to work, God did not intend for man to have a free ride. In Proverbs 21:25 it says, ***"The desire of the lazy man kills him, for his hands refuse to labor."*** Ecclesiastes 9:10 says, ***"Whatever your hand finds to do, do it with your might."***

"Well," we say, "I want a day job behind a desk. I don't want to work in a factory!" First of all, there's nothing wrong with factory work. Believe it or not, there are some folks who enjoy working in factories. Many blue collar jobs pay very well and provide good benefits.

One of the Bible's strongest commands concerning work is found in 1 Timothy 5:8 where it says, "But if anyone does not provide for his own, *and especially for those of his household*, **he has denied the faith and is worse than an unbeliever**." Of course, we all want to do something we enjoy — something we can put our hearts into. But, should our first priority be the *type of job* we have, or should it be *providing* for those of our household?

What if we desire a white collar day job? What will we do until we're prepared and ready for that type of position? We may have to work at jobs we don't particularly enjoy to provide for our family until we find the job we desire. However, we must be prepared because that process may take time. We may have to start out at an entry level position and work our way upward. Or, we may have to go back to school and increase our knowledge and skill.

God makes it clear in His Word that we *must work* if we are going to be pleasing to Him. If we develop good work habits they will serve us well. When an able-bodied person is too lazy to work, no one benefits. He suffers, his family suffers, and those who are truly in need suffer.

Ephesians 4:28 tells us, *"Let him who stole steal no longer,* ***but rather let him labor, working with his hands*** *what is good, that he may have something to give him who has need."* God wants us to labor, not only so we can provide for those of our own house, but also so we can have something to give to those in need.

Consider the Ant!

A guest speaker I invited to speak at my church told this story: A man saw an ant crawling across his living room floor. He took a stick from his fireplace and interrupted the ant's journey. The man put the stick in the path of the ant and the ant crawled on to the stick.

He held the stick in the air and when the ant reached one end of the stick he switched hands. The ant never missed a step, simply crawling back and forth on the stick as the man held it in his hand. Finally, the man tired of torturing the poor ant and put the ant back down on the floor.

When the man put the ant back down on the floor he placed the stick several feet away from the ant's original path. Then, he noticed something. Without missing a beat, the ant walked right back to it's original path, and picked up where he left off. You see, ants follow a scent trail. And even though the ant was detoured, when released the ant immediately got back on track.

> *Go to the ant, you sluggard! Consider her ways, and be wise,*
>
> *Which having no captain, overseer or ruler,*
>
> *Provides her supplies in the summer, and gathers her food in the harvest.*
>
> *How long will you slumber, O sluggard? When will you rise from your sleep?*
>
> *A little sleep, a little slumber, a little folding of the hands to sleep —*
>
> *So shall your poverty come on you like a prowler, and your need like an armed man.*
>
> *Proverbs 6:6-11*

How about us? Are we easily detoured in life? Or, do we seek direction from God and stay on track? Maybe we identify more with this scenario:

Boss to tardy employee: "You're twenty minutes late again! Don't you know what time our people start work here?"

Employee: "No sir, they've always already started by the time I get here."[3]

According to Proverbs, the ant has "no captain." In other words, she doesn't have a supervisor ant having to stand over her shoulder to make sure she's doing her work. She works hard while being unsupervised. She's diligent to work until the job is done. No matter what kind of job we're at, we will find that quality of character is rare — someone who works hard while unsupervised, and works diligently until the job is completed.

Many of us know what it's like to get *comfortable* in a job. Basically, we discover where the line is we cannot

---

[3] *Parables Etc.*, February 1991, submitted by Kenneth L. Dodge

cross. Then instead of continuing to push ourselves to excel (as most of us do when we're new employees) we get in a comfort zone where we put out just enough energy and effort to get by.

Of course, not everyone gets in a comfort zone. There are some who continually push themselves to excel. It's not uncommon to find that the majority of employees accuse the motivated people of "bucking for a promotion."

The truth of the matter is, the motivated ones are rocking the boat and making everyone else look bad. Sluggards don't like that! So the sluggards do their best to turn up the old peer pressure so Johnny Motivation will slow down. That attitude, *especially for Christians*, is absolutely wrong!

It's not unlike the boss who approached one of his ambitious men and told him, "I've had my eye on you. You're a hard worker and you've put in long hours. You're very ambitious."

"Thank you," replied the employee.

But the boss added, "So, consequently, I'm going to fire you. It's men like you who start competing companies."[4]

What else does the ant do? She's always *working the season*. When it's summertime she provides supplies, and when it's harvest she gathers food. What happens if springtime arrives but the farmer sleeps in every morning neglecting to prepare the soil and plant his crop? Then, all of a sudden, he realizes his foolishness and gets busy plowing at the beginning of summer. Now, he's out of season.

---

[4] *Christian Clippings,* submitted by Michael Kelley in Parables Etc., October 1988

If you've ever lived in farm country you've heard the expression, "knee high by the fourth of July." Farmers want their corn to be at least up to their knees by the fourth of July. If it's been a good Spring, the corn has usually grown above "knee high." My point is that there are certain signs during the growing season that will indicate whether their crops are on track, and whether or not they might have a good harvest. If a farmer wants his crops to be on track he cannot afford to be lazy.

Proverbs 28:19 says, *"He who tills his land will have plenty of bread, but he who follows frivolity will have poverty enough!"* We cannot be a sluggard in life and expect to accomplish anything worthwhile. We can dream of success all we want, but: *"a little sleep, a little slumber, a little folding of the hands to sleep, and so shall your poverty come on you like a prowler."* **Laziness is destined to overtake the sluggard and wheedle him into poverty.**

Frank Outlaw said, "Watch your actions; they become habits. Watch your habits; they become character. Watch your character; it becomes your destiny." Thomas Edison said, "Show me a thoroughly satisfied man, and I will show you a failure."

Common sense tells us we all need to take care of ourselves physically. I'm talking about proper rest, proper diet, and recreation. At the same time, I also believe we need to push ourselves to excel. Proverbs 13:4 tells us, *"The soul of a lazy man desires, and has nothing; **but the soul of the diligent shall be made rich."*** A lazy man can desire or dream about having wealth, but if he remains lazy that's all it will ever be — a dream.

Like other things we do in life, hard work can become a habit. We need to keep it in balance so we don't work ourselves to an early grave. However, it is important for ourselves and our families to work hard and excel at what we do. Proverbs 22:29 says it all, *"Do you see a man who excels in his work? He will stand before kings; He will not stand before unknown men."*

WE MUST CHOOSE TO EXCEL!

Chapter 4

Cross Those Bridges!

"We are told never to cross a bridge till we come to it, but this world is owned by men who have crossed bridges in their imagination far ahead of the crowd." — Speakers Library

Vision is the essence of a life full of purpose and meaning. Of course I'm not talking about our natural sight, or vision. Many blind people have had great "vision" and made lasting imprints on our society. Helen Keller is one of the most famous. Helen Keller once said, "The most pathetic person in the world is someone who has sight, but no vision."

Of course, I'm talking about the kind of insight that gives deeper meaning to our life. The type of vision that sparks a sense of destiny and drives us toward that destiny like a hungry lion stalking its prey.

Woodrow Wilson said, "No man that does not see visions will ever realize any high hope or undertake any high enterprise." A true sense of purpose and vision for the future will cause us to get up every morning full of hope, and make the most of our day. It puts a fire in our eyes and gives us an unquenchable hunger to run our race.

If we will allow ourselves to become immersed in God's plans for our lives (plans based upon God's Word), and connect our human will (our motivation and drive) with godly pursuits, the devil will not be able to stop us. Godly vision + Our willingness and obedience + The magnificent Spirit of God = Success.

I have often wondered why so many people live their lives without hope and without vision. Is it bad teaching (doctrine) that has stolen their hope? Is it some bad circumstance in their lives that has stripped away their sense of purpose? Is it their parental upbringing that robbed them of any hope for the future? I pray that this book will help instill hope and good doctrine to all those who have been deprived of these essentials.

Here are a few things we must do:

1. Introduce Ourselves to Change

There are people who simply have a difficult time accepting the idea of change. Think about this: In 1803, the British created a civil service position in a which a man was required to stand on the cliffs of Dover with a spy glass. His job was to be on the lookout for invasion. He was to ring a bell if he saw the army of Napoleon Bonaparte approaching. That job was not eliminated until 1945!

Change is God's idea. In 2 Corinthians 3:18, it says, *"But we all, with unveiled face, beholding as in a mirror the glory of the Lord, are being transformed* [changed] *into the same image from glory to glory, just as by the Spirit of the Lord."* If we will look into the Word of God (the mirror) with complete honesty (unveiled face), and continuously (every day) behold the glory of the Lord (through study of the Bible, prayer, and heartfelt worship), the Spirit of the Lord will begin to help transform us into the image that we are beholding.

The Word of God is a mirror that reflects the image of the Lord. If we will allow the Spirit of God to work in our lives, burning out everything that does not reflect the revealed image of Christ, then we will be changed from glory to glory! But, we must be willing to change.

"There are three things we know about the future: 1) it is not going to be like the past, 2) it is not going to be exactly the way we think it's going to be, and 3) the rate of change will take place faster than we imagine."[5] That is certainly true of the times we're living in! Knowledge is literally overtaking knowledge. Almost as soon as new computer software is introduced it's outdated.

Get excited about change! We all love to be surprised with gifts at Christmas time. We love to buy new things to entertain us. But, let one new thing pop up in our lives unannounced and we go berserk! Or, heaven forbid, let the pastor change something in the church. If that happens to us we should avoid looking foolish like a long-time member of a church who scolded his new pastor for his radical new ideas and changes: "Reverend" he said, "If God were alive today, He would be shocked at the changes in this church!"[6]

---

[5] John Mason, *An Enemy Called Average,* 1990.

[6] *Christian Leadership Letter,* by World Vision, February 1982.

This is not the time to sit on our God-given seat cushion and enjoy the view. Besides, what fun would life be without a little mystery and a few new challenges? I believe as busy as these times are that we can still be at peace in our souls. However, there is so much work to be done, and as Jesus said, "*...the laborers are few.*" We can't be sidelined by an unwillingness to change. Will Rogers said, "Even if you're on the right track, you'll get run over if you just sit there."

2. Check Yourself Out

In one of Charles Schultz's *Peanuts* comic strips, Snoopy the dog is sitting by the side of the road, watching all the kids going by. Snoopy is reflecting to himself. He says, "I wonder why it is that some were born people, and others were born dogs. It just isn't fair." And then in the last frame he concludes, "Why was I the lucky one?"

How do you see yourself? What gifts, talents, or callings has God given you? I have asked people that question before and some will say, *very adamantly,* "God didn't give me any gifts or talents!" Then, the next thing you know they're sitting at a computer, clicking away with ease, putting normal computer users to shame. Or, another will be out in the parking lot of the workplace helping fix a car while explaining all the intricacies of the 5.0 liter fuel-injected high performance turbo V8. So many people have God-given gifts, talents, or callings right under their noses, but fail to recognize them.

Mike Murdock said, "What generates passion and zeal in you is a clue to revealing your destiny. What you love is a clue to something you contain." Who do we think put that passion in us? Where did it come from? Fluke of nature? No! God wants to use us, and He has placed in us all the abilities we need to accomplish the task. For most people, their gifts and abilities can be easily by the time they're out of high school. Thos abilities need to be nurtured and encouraged tc . ..iop.

Proverbs 18:16 says, *"A man's gift makes room for him, and brings him before great men."* First Samuel 16:14 tells of a distressing spirit that was troubling King Saul. In verse 16 of that chapter it says, *"Let our master now command your servants, who are before you, to seek out a man who is a skillful player on the harp."* The servants of Saul sought after a man who could play skillfully. A man who was a talented musician and who when he played, the distressing spirit would leave Saul.

In verse 18 of 1 Samuel 16, it says, *"Then one of the servants answered and said, "Look, I have seen a son of Jesse the Bethlehemite* [David]*, who is skillful in playing, a mighty man of valor, a man of war, prudent in speech, and a handsome person; and the Lord is with him."* And so it was, whenever a distressing spirit was on Saul, he would call for David. David would play his harp and the distressing spirit would leave Saul.

What were David's qualifications? Did he have a Ph.D. in rocket science? No, David started out in life as a sheep herder! As David's skills surfaced they appeared to be extreme opposites. He was *skillful in playing his harp*, and a *man of war*. A man of war? How did they know? The David and Goliath incident hadn't happened yet. They must have heard about David killing the lion and the bear that had attacked his father's sheep. Even with these strange and varied qualifications, King Saul still called for David. David's gift made a way for him and he stood before a king.

Also notice the servants told King Saul that David was *prudent in speech*, and *a handsome person*. Hidden in that verse are two great keys to success. Prudent in speech means that David *thought* before he spoke. He chose his words carefully.

We need to be careful in choosing our words. Many times it can mean the difference between success and failure. Think of how many lawsuits are waged over someone's angry, slanderous words. Think of how many political careers have been ruined by misspoken words. Think about these words which actually appeared in a church bulletin: "The ladies of the church have cast off clothing of every kind, and they may be seen in the church basement on Friday afternoon." Wouldn't we rather be known as David was: a person who is "prudent in speech?"

David was also a handsome person. Webster's defines "handsome" as of fine, or admirable appearance. Thank God beauty is in the eye of the beholder! Nevertheless, despite our lot in life concerning our comeliness, we can all do our best to look nice. At the very least we can look "admirable."

As ambassadors of Christ, we should always make an effort to put our best foot forward. If we go to the bank to get a loan for a new business venture, even if we don't have a brand-new suit, it usually doesn't cost an arm and a leg to look presentable. We shouldn't let our loan officer or prospective employer see us come in with unwashed, uncombed hair, wearing holey blue jeans and a tie-dye T-shirt. Because, unless we're getting a loan from Vito the loan shark, or applying for a job in Color My World Tattoo Parlor, they probably won't be very impressed.

We need to be honest with ourselves. We need to identify the gifts that God has given us, and begin to develop those gifts with excellence so that we can use them to the glory of God. We need to display our God-given gifts skillfully by being prudent in our speech and admirable in our appearance.

Dreams are Free

Have you ever had a vision for something — a project or business venture — only to be stopped dead in your tracks with nowhere to go? The disappointment of failure can lead to depression, which is only a half step away from hopelessness. The good news is that you're not alone! Thousands of successful people have failed many times before all the pieces of success fell into place.

Think about this: Eli Whitney was laughed at when he showed his cotton gin. Edison had to install his electric light free of charge in an office building before anyone would even look at it. The first sewing machine was smashed to pieces by a Boston mob. People scoffed at the idea of railroads. People thought that traveling thirty miles an hour would stop the circulation of the blood. Morse had to plead before ten Congresses before they would even look at his telegraph.

We can't give up on our *God-given* dreams! If God has ordained it to be, it will happen. The only thing that stops our God-given dreams and visions is us. It costs nothing to have vision and it costs even less to dream. But, in order for our dreams and visions to become reality it will take diligence, effort, and most importantly, a firm trust and reliance in God and His Word. We have to realize, of course, that it's possible that other people will not understand our vision. Just remember, they're not seeing the world through our eyes.

One day, Michelangelo saw a block of marble which the owner said was of no value. "It is valuable to me," said Michelangelo. "There is an angel imprisoned in it, and I must set it free." You know there had to be folks in Michelangelo's day who thought he was loony. "Hey, look at crazy Mike over there! He's carrying home another piece of marble! Let's call him Marbleangelo!" And, what about Jesus? His people thought so much of Him they crucified Him!

We all know of someone who simply gave up on their vision. Perhaps they even slipped into a state of hopelessness. When depression sets in it can get a little scary! Proverbs 13:12 explains this very plainly: *"Hope deferred makes the heart sick, but when the desire comes, it is a tree of life."*

The good news is that God has a plan for our life. We *never* have to be without hope. Jeremiah 29:11-13 reads: *"For I know the thoughts that I think toward you, says the Lord, thoughts of peace and not of evil,* ***to give you a future and a hope.*** *Then, you will call upon Me and go and pray to Me, and I will listen to you. And you will seek Me and find Me,* ***when you search for Me with all your heart."***

A true sense of vision and purpose for our lives emerges as we spend time in the presence of God. Proverbs 29:18 says, *"Where there is no revelation* [prophetic vision — word from God], *the people cast off restraint."* In other words, where there is no godly direction concerning vision and purpose people go their own ways and do whatever they think is right. However, Jeremiah 29:13 tells us, *"And you will seek Me and find Me, when you search for Me with all your heart."*

Psalm 37:4-5 says, *"Delight yourself also in the Lord, and He shall give you the desires of your heart. Commit your way to the Lord, trust also in Him, and He shall bring it to pass."* Notice that there are two obvious keys in that verse to seeing vision and dreams fulfilled: 1) delighting ourselves in the Lord, and 2) committing our ways to the Lord.

There is absolutely no reason to be hopeless when we know God. If we're not close to God **we can** get close to Him! How? What do we do if we want to develop into the best basketball player we can possibly be? We shoot baskets with the best basketball players we can find! We play with people who push us to excel. What I'm saying is find someone who has a close relationship with God and hang out with them! Go to church with them! Go to prayer meetings with them! Ask questions, and talk about the Bible with them! Isn't that what we do in other areas of our lives when we want something very badly?

What do you dream about? For what do you have a vision? Maybe it's a vision for your family. Maybe it's a dream of opening a business. Maybe you dream of teaching children. Whatever it may be, if it's a godly vision and you want God's help to bring it to reality, you must first delight yourself in the Lord and commit your way to Him. Then, find people with the same passion and talk with them, discuss issues, and most of all *pray*.

We can't *ever* stop dreaming or lose hope! If we feel all hope is gone, we need to go directly to God's Word. Then, we need to spend time in prayer communicating with the Father. And finally, we need to spend time with fellow believers who will help stir up those God-given dreams and visions, and encourage us to pursue God with all our heart.

REFUSE TO GIVE UP UNTIL YOU HAVE ACCOMPLISHED WHAT GOD HAS CALLED YOU TO DO!

Chapter 5

I Love It! I Love It! I Want More of It!

The longer I live, the more I realize the impact of attitude on life. Attitude, to me, is more important than facts. It is more important than the past, than education, than money, than circumstances, than failures, than successes, than what other people think or say or do. It is more important than appearance, giftedness, or skill. It will make or break a company — a church — a home.

The remarkable thing is we have a choice everyday regarding the attitude we will embrace for that day. We cannot change our past...we cannot change the fact that people will act in a certain way. We cannot change the inevitable. The only thing we can do is play on the one string we have, and that is our attitude.

I am convinced that life is 10% what happens to me and 90% how I react to it. And so it is with you — we are in charge of our attitudes.
— Charles Swindoll

After we had all loaded onto the "cattle truck" we began to roll down the street toward our new home. All forty young men sat silent not even daring to look at the tall man wearing a "Smokey the Bear" hat. He told us to repeat these words, *"Practice makes perfect, and pay attention to detail."* We repeated those words all the way to our destination.

When we arrived at our company street, the doors to the truck flew open and the tall man began to yell at us, "Get movin'! What's a matter with you pukes — you're movin' too slow!" And that was just the beginning of Army basic training.

Up until that point in my life, Army basic training was the most difficult thing I had encountered. The title to this chapter came from my not so fond memories of bayonet training. During bayonet training we would simulate three bayonet thrusts while shouting, "Kill! Kill! Kill!" Then, the drill instructor would call us to attention. As the entire platoon snapped to attention we would shout in unison, **"I love it! I love it! I want more of it! Hurt me drill sergeant, hurt me, huh!"** Isn't that uplifting?

It may not be uplifting now, but in Basic Training it was very motivating. It was part of the drill instructor's job to keep us motivated. We all need people in our lives to help keep us energized. Proverbs 27:17 says, *"As iron sharpens iron, so a man sharpens the countenance of his friend."*

Who keeps you motivated? Your spouse? Your pastor? Your best buddy? We must keep the fire alive within us so that we will pursue God and His plans will all our heart. We can have great vision, big dreams, *but without passion our dreams will die*. Let's take a look at where that kind of passion comes from.

You Must Believe In Yourself!

At first we may think that to *believe in ourselves* is a very humanistic point of view. Very introspective. Very philosophical. It sounds like we all need to be sitting on pillows in a coffeehouse banging on bongos and snapping our fingers. Or, it sounds like something guru Rashim Mishmash would whisper to us while sitting cross-legged on top of Mt. Imablowhard. But, think about this statement by Zig Ziglar: **"You can't consistently perform in a manner that is inconsistent with the way you see yourself."**

I remember quite a few young men who dropped out of Army basic training because they had convinced themselves they couldn't make it through. I also remember others who were on the verge of quitting, but all it took was some encouraging words to help convince them they could complete the training.

Many times as a police officer, I heard frustrated parents tell their children, "You're no good! You're gonna wind up in prison just like your daddy!" So often the words spoken over those children came to pass because no one ever convinced them otherwise. Sadly, there are many young people who are involuntarily shoved onto the road leading to failure, and they become convinced that's where they belong.

It is within us to modify our attitudes and develop a confidence *based upon what God has to say about us.* I'm talking about the part of our attitude called self-confidence. I don't believe the term *self-confidence* is inconsistent with the biblical principles of meekness and humility.

When I say "self-confidence," I don't mean having confidence **in our own abilities,** but instead having confidence **in Christ who is in you, the hope of glory**. (See Colossians 1:27.) We *can* increase our confidence in the ability *of the One who is in us*, and that confidence must be intermingled with meekness and humility in order to produce godly results.

Philippians 1:6 says, **"Being confident of this very thing**, *that He* who has begun a good work in you *will complete it* until the day of Jesus Christ." And then Philippians 4:13, Paul says, "I can do all things *through Christ who strengthens me*." Notice it's **through Christ** that we can do all things.

Self-confidence becomes inappropriate (and downright ugly) when we flaunt our gifts and abilities as if we are the greatest thing since hot-dogs on a stick. *That's when we begin relying on the flesh and not the power and anointing of God.* It also begins to expose the pride and arrogance in our hearts, which is a stench in the nostrils of God! The problem is, at that point we've forgotten *with whom* all our gifts and abilities originate, and *for whose glory* they were meant. Philippians 3:3 tells us that **we are to have no confidence in the flesh**. Proverbs 16:18 says, *"Pride goes before destruction, and a haughty spirit before a fall."*

As Christians, our "self-confidence" must be rooted and grounded in what the Word of God has to say about us, and in our assurance of God's power to perform His Word. Much like a little boy who once prayed: "Dear God, please take care of my daddy and my mommy and my sister and my brother and my doggy and me. Oh, and please take care of yourself, God. If anything happens to You, we're gonna be in a big mess."[7]

In Proverbs 3:21-26 (speaking of godly wisdom) it says, *"My son, let them not depart from your eyes — keep sound wisdom and discretion; So they will be life to your soul and grace to your neck. Then you will walk safely in your way, and your foot will not stumble. When you lie down, you will not be afraid; Yes, you will lie down and your sleep will be sweet. Do not be afraid of sudden terror, nor of trouble from the wicked when it comes;* ***For the Lord will be your confidence,*** *and will keep your foot from being caught."*

> ***In the fear of the Lord there is strong confidence****, and His children will have a place of refuge.*
>
> *Proverbs 14:26*

Before Moses died, God directed him to commission Joshua to lead the people of Israel. Joshua had an enormous task awaiting him. God encouraged Joshua by saying, *"No man shall be able to stand before you all the days of your life; as I was with Moses, so I will be with you. I will not leave you nor forsake you. Be strong and of good courage, for to this people you shall divide as an inheritance the land which I swore to their fathers to give them. Only be strong and very courageous."* As God continues in Joshua 1, He tells Joshua another time to be "strong and of good courage." (See Joshua 1:5-7,9.)

Can you see that God wants us to have confidence? Question: What is our confidence based upon? *"Being confident that He will complete it..." "I can do all things*

---

[7] No source available.

through Christ..." "For the Lord will be your confidence..." "In the fear of the Lord is strong confidence..." "I will not leave you nor forsake you..." Our *self-confidence* must be firmly established in God's ability and not the ability of our flesh (our own natural strength). Then what we're truly saying is, **"Any confidence I have is only because I'm confident in the ability and the power of God."**

Passion Fuels Our Dreams

What motivated the Wright Brothers to build a flying machine? Who convinced them they could fly? And why would a man named Thomas Edison devote years of his life and baskets of money, pursuing wild ideas like the light bulb? Where did those crazy ideas come from?

Those crazy ideas came as their imaginations were tickled by bits and pieces of information gained from something they read, something they heard, something they observed, something they touched, something they smelled, or a combination thereof. How do I know? I know because we're all human, and God created our imaginations to be stimulated by our five physical senses. And, as children of God, our creative abilities are also inspired by the Spirit of God. (See Jeremiah 33:3, Daniel 2:47, and Job 32:8.)

Obviously I wasn't alive during those great golden years of genuinely novel inventions (surprise, surprise), but I believe I can safely say that those extraordinary inventions (that literally changed the world) would have never been birthed into existence unless the inventors *passionately* pursued their dreams.

It's not unlike a master mechanic with his nose in a big, thick, Chilton's Auto Manual soaking up all the information that's necessary to get a vehicle purring like a kitten. Or, an architect bent studiously over his drawing board refusing to quit until he figures out how to add that final artistic touch to the building that will be his crowning achievement.

Webster's defines "passion" as any kind of feeling or emotion, as hope, fear, joy, grief, anger, love, desire, etc., *especially when of compelling force;* **strong amorous feeling of desire.**

Where should a *Christian's* passion to pursue their dreams come from? Whether it's a vision for some type of ministry, invention, or business, what motivates a man or woman of God to run after that vision? What *manual* do they stick their nose in that not only gives them the knowledge to run their race, but also the courage and inward strength to complete the task?

The Word of God is not only the foundation and building block for everything a Christian believes, but it also calls us to press on toward our God-inspired destiny. The Word of God is what instructs us and motivates us to conduct ourselves in a *Christ-like manner*, so that our faith in the Word of God will produce godly results, thereby bringing our God-given dreams to their fruition. **In other words, the Bible provides us with all the tools we need to accomplish the task.**

God's Word is where all doctrine (teaching) concerning our life with God should be taken from. In 2 Timothy 3:14-17, it says, *"But you must continue in the things which you have learned and been assured of, knowing from whom you have learned them, and that from childhood you have known the Holy Scriptures, which are able to make you wise for salvation through faith which is in Christ Jesus.* ***All Scripture is given by inspiration of God****, and is profitable for doctrine, for reproof, for* *correction, for instruction in righteousness,* ***that the man of God may be complete, thoroughly equipped for every good work."***

Follow me on this: Psalm 138:2 tells us, *"...For You have magnified Your word above all Your name."* Then, Isaiah 40:8 says, *"The grass withers, the flower fades,* ***but the Word of our God stands forever."*** Psalm 119:160 tells us that, ***"The entirety of Your word is truth."*** Romans 10:17 tells us how we receive faith — *"So then faith comes by hearing, and hearing by the word of God."* And, Hebrews 11:6 teaches us that, ***"...without faith it is impossible to please Him,*** *for he who comes to God must believe that* ***He is****, and that* ***He is a rewarder*** *of those who diligently seek Him."*

So here's what we know from Scripture:

1. **God Himself** has declared (through his apostles, prophets, etc.) that His Word (all scripture) was given supernaturally by *His inspiration*;
2. Everything we need for doctrine, reproof, correction, and instruction in righteousness *is in the Bible;*
3. If we receive it and put it into practice we will be equipped for *every good work*;
4. God magnifies His Word *above His name;*
5. His Word will *stand forever*;
6. The entirety of His Word *is truth;*
7. We receive faith (a firm trust and reliance in God) by *hearing the Word of God;*
8. And, that **without faith** (a firm trust and reliance in God) **it is impossible to please Him** *because* we will not truly believe that He exists, or that He will do what His Word says He will do.

Really, it's a pretty simple equation. The fact that we not only need a knowledge of the Word of God, but also *a love for it* seems obvious. God magnifies His Word above His own name! The reason for that is because God, *who has been around a little while,* is smart enough to know that a person is only as good as His Word. If God's Word had no substance or power to it, people would not believe in Him (and vice versa). God will not only perform His Word, but He also tells us that **it will not pass away** (just like Him)!

To truly be motivated and passionate about pursuing what God has called you to do with your life you must believe that God's Word is true, and that He will do all that is written in it. **The entirety of His Word is truth!** Not to mention that we **cannot** please God without faith! Why? Trying to please God without faith would be similar to my son coming up to me and asking me to give him five dollars. Then, turning around to his sister and saying, "I don't believe dad can, *or* that he will give me five dollars." How would that make me feel as a father? We must not only demonstrate a firm trust and reliance in the existence of God, but also that God *will* reward those who *diligently seek Him*.

Remember, faith comes by *hearing the Word*. So not only is hearing teaching from God's Word important, but also developing a hunger for the Word of God in our own personal lives. The passion and the drive for pursuing our *God-inspired dreams and destiny* is a product of spending time studying God's Word. This happens because the more we get to know Him personally, and develop a strong faith in Him, the more we will realize that *with God all things are possible*. (See Mark 9:23.)

John Mason said, "Nothing significant was ever achieved without passion." Passion is that part of us that drives us to pursue the manifestation of our dreams. It's what keeps us up at night thinking, planning, and organizing. It causes us to lose sleep and even give up a meal or two until we have put one more piece of the puzzle in its proper place. It causes us to devour information concerning what we're trying to accomplish. We keep our passion for our dreams alive by spending time with God and His Word. Because, **passion is what fuels the fire of our dreams**.

Let Your Flesh Cry Out!

Can we think of something in our life we have an intense passion about? For some it's sports. I have known people who get downright depressed if their favorite sports team loses. As for me, I can get the same feeling when God is not the motivating factor or the heartfelt passion of my life that He ought to be.

If we examine the lives of the great heroes of our faith, we will find that they not only knew the Word of God, *and obeyed it*, but they also had a passion and *reverence* for the very presence of God Himself. That passion for God not only creates a burning desire inside of us to be pleasing to God, but it also drives us to pursue the dreams God has given us. **Great Christian exploits are born out of a passion for the Word of God, and a passion for the presence of God.**

If a Christian is going to have a passion for the things God has commissioned him to do, he must also develop a passion *for God Himself*. What do I mean by a passion for God Himself? David (a great hero of our faith), quite obviously had a passion for God. In Psalm 84:2, David said, *"My soul longs, **yes, even faints for the courts of the Lord; my heart and my flesh cry out for the living***

***God.*"** We need to ask ourselves: Do we have that type of passion for the presence of God?

How do we develop a passion for God? There are many ways. One way is to BE INVOLVED IN OUR LOCAL CHURCH! Jesus is the head of the Church. (See Ephesians 1:22.) And, the Church is His body. (See Ephesians 5:30.) I guess it stands to reason, then, if we desire to have fellowship with the **head of the Church**, we must have fellowship with **His body**. Moreover, if we want to be a part of Him then be a part of His body. How can we say that we love the head of the Church, but do not love His body?

All throughout the New Testament, Christians are referred to as brothers and sisters in Christ. Those who call Jesus their Lord and believe that He rose from the dead, are brothers and sisters in the body of Christ. We need to get involved with our spiritual family and be a part of what God is doing in our local church! Being involved in our local church *should* add stability to our walk with God which, in turn, not only plays a major role in our day-to-day life, but also in our future.

Another way is to FELLOWSHIP WITH OTHER BELIEVERS. Remember, Proverbs 27:17 said, *"As iron sharpens iron, so a man sharpens the countenance of a friend."* We need to get with someone who has a passion for the Word of God and discuss the Bible. We should discuss issues *without* arguing! We need to discuss the Bible with the intention of gaining an understanding of the scriptures and challenging one another to grow in the Word of God. There's nothing I love more than having a good, intense discussion about the Bible.

When we develop and continue in our passion for the Word of God, it will not only take us deeper in our personal relationship with God, but it will also help us develop strong Christian relationships. These relationships will be strong because they're not based upon worldly ideals, but upon everlasting principles. Strong relationships with brothers and sisters in Christ are an essential part of pursuing God's will for our lives.

Finally, DEVELOP A PASSION FOR WORSHIPPING GOD. Psalm 99:5 tells us to, *"Exalt the Lord our God, and worship at His footstool —* ***He is holy.*** *"* The Hebrew word for worship used there is *shachah*, and means to bow, to stoop; to bow down before someone as an act of submission or reverence; to worship; to fall or bow down when paying homage to God. The primary meaning is to make oneself low. In this reference *shachah* is used in contrast to exaltation; exalt the Lord (lift Him up high) and worship (bow yourselves down low before Him) at the place of His feet. (See James Strong's Concordance.)

Worshipping God *with all our hearts* has always been, and always will be, one of the greatest keys to living close to the heart of God. We must develop a taste for passionate, heartfelt worship. We need to cultivate in our hearts a strong passion and desire for the courts of the Lord. We need to worship God at His footstool until every time we're away from that "secret place" (Psalm 91), our hearts and our flesh will cry out for the courts of the Lord. It's the only addiction in life that will produce peace, joy, revelation, and godly direction.

Has God has given you a dream and a vision for your life? Lay those dreams and visions at His footstool, and allow the Creator to speak to you. Allow Him to reveal to your heart, supernatural insights concerning your dreams, so that He may continually guide your footsteps and stir a passion inside you so that you may advance in strength and power.

> *But those who wait* [to wait for, to look for, expect, hope] *on the Lord shall renew their strength; they shall mount up with wings like eagles, they shall run and not be weary, they shall walk and not faint.*
>
> *Isaiah 40:31*

Psalm 37:4-5 tell us that **if we delight ourselves in the Lord**, He will give us the desires of our heart, *and* if we **commit our ways to the Lord** and trust in Him, *He will bring it to pass.*

We need to allow the Spirit of God to instill a confidence in us that's rooted in meekness and humility! We should continually be inspired and motivated by the very words of our Creator! A passion for *God Himself* should be at the center of our lives! When we worship God daily, read His Word, and give Him a place of honor in our lives by obeying His commands, **He** will see to it that we succeed. He cannot help Himself.

LET YOUR PASSION FOR PURSUING YOUR DREAMS FLOW FROM THE VERY THRONE OF GOD.

Chapter 6

Just Do It!

When Hernando de Soto landed his expedition on the shores of Florida, he sent a small party back to the ships to set them ablaze. His confused men watched from the water's edge in horrified disbelief as puffs of billowing smoke swirled into the air. De Soto turned to his men and said, "Gentlemen, you are home." [8]

I've burned bridges before (only figuratively), but I don't believe I've ever had someone else burn them for me. In the last two chapters. we've discussed two very important components to success — Vision and Passion.

---

[8] *The Rest of Your Life,* by Patrick M. Morley — Thomas Nelson Publishing, 1992.

We must envision it with our mind's eye, then have the passion to pursue our dreams.

I've known many people who have both vision and passion. Their passion may even be coupled with natural gifts and abilities. However, far too many people fail to take the first step in literal pursuit of their dreams. Henry Ford said, "We can't build a reputation on what we're *going* to do." I agree with the late great four-wheeled mogul except to say that **we will** build a reputation. Our reputation will be *that we're all talk, and no walk.*

Nehemiah had vision and passion. What would have happened if he had never taken the first step in rebuilding Jerusalem's wall? (See the book of Nehemiah.)

Most of us can think of someone we know personally who has God-given talents, abilities, and dreams. More than likely they're even very passionate when they discuss their dreams, yet they never move out beyond discussion. We have to put some walkin' to our talkin'.

Theodore Roosevelt said, "Far better it is to dare mighty things, to win glorious triumphs, even though checked by failure, than to rank with those poor spirits who neither enjoy much nor suffer much because they live in the gray twilight that knows not victory or defeat."

As another man once said, "If we don't have goals in our life, we will never be able to tell if we're a failure." I would take it one step further and say, "If we don't include *action* with our goals, we will never be able to tell if we're a failure."

A poster was displayed in a conference room at IMI (computers and disc-drives manufacturer). It shows two or three large, ponderous hippopotami standing around with their gigantic mouths wide open. The words on the poster read, "When all is said and done, more is said than done." [9] Let's not be gigantic, ponderous hippopotami!

Where's the Starting Gate?

First of all — pray. Have you taken the time to discern what **God's will** is for your life? You may say, "But I don't know how to discern God's will!" God not only gives each of us gifts and talents, but He also gives us desires that coincide with them. Has God given you a desire to teach? Maybe your gifts and abilities lie under the hood of a car? You might possibly have a desire to be a physician or a psychologist? I'm simply saying that if you look closely at yourself, you'll discover your God-given gifts.

Once we uncover our dreams, abilities, and goals, then we must lay out a plan. For instance, we shouldn't go to the local junior college and enroll in a political science degree program if our heart's desire is to be a plumber. It would make more sense to find a trade school, or become an apprentice with Sanford Biggs (your uncle Joe's best buddy) who's a plumber. We shouldn't frustrate ourselves with meaningless, and sometimes endless side journeys. Instead, zero in on our goal and set a course! Then, we begin moving in that direction and don't stop until we've reached our goal!

We must also strike a balance between *our dreams and reality*. If we have a dream to be a concert pianist, but every piano teacher we've ever studied with has dropped us because they say we couldn't play the piano even if we had four hands, the piano only had one ivory key, and every song was written with that one note, then maybe

---

[9] Source unknown.

we need to reconsider. Maybe we truly are the next Bach or Beethoven and nobody recognizes it. But, maybe not.

There's nothing wrong with taking the road less traveled. That's very admirable. We need to keep this in mind though, if we choose to take that road, then we must be prepared for all the hills and bumps that are ahead of us. Although, if we're simply not being honest with ourselves, then we must do some serious soul searching to find that middle ground between starry-eyed dreams and reality. Sometimes we just need to sit down in front of a mirror and be brutally honest with the person looking back at us.

Each of us are unique and God has made us for a purpose. God Himself tells us in Jeremiah 29:11, " For I know the plans I have for you, declares the Lord, plans to prosper you, plans to give you a future and a hope." God's not trying to keep it a secret. Let's pray and ask God for guidance if we're not sure what direction to take. God wants us to know and follow His plan for our life. If we're seeking after God, we'll not only find Him, but He will direct our paths.

Proverbs 8:17-18 says this about wisdom, *"I love those who love me, and those who seek me diligently will find me. Riches and honor are with me, enduring riches and righteousness."* True wisdom comes from God, and if we seek after it we will find it. Most of all, trust in God! A lot of successful people have!

If At First We Don't Succeed...

Surely we know what's coming next — Try, Try Again! Proverbs 24:16 says, *"For a righteous man may fall seven times and rise again..."* What do we do if we get bucked off a horse? We get right back on! Or, we do like I did when I was a child and chase the horse down (or pony in my case) and jump back on!

A very wealthy man was once asked, “What’s the secret to your success?”

The wealthy man replied, “You must always make the right decisions.”

The wealthy man was questioned a second time, “How do you learn to make the right decisions?”

The wealthy man replied, “I learned by making wrong decisions.”

Mistakes generally result in experience, but wisdom comes through the proper application of acquired knowledge.

As we work God’s plan for our lives, day in and day out, we will undoubtedly make mistakes. Yet, as we trust God while “putting our hand to the plow,” we will gain wisdom as we move toward our destiny. We’ll learn what to do, and what **not** to do. We can’t get discouraged in our trials and errors. Most of us learn better by doing rather than watching. Benjamin Franklin said, “Tell me and I’ll forget; teach me, and I might remember; **involve me, and I’ll learn**.” If there is no action to our beliefs, no experience is gained, and therefore, no wisdom is acquired for future application.

We need to get our eyeballs off our failures, and focus them on success! See failures as what they are — Learning experiences — Hurdles in the track of life — Small puddles leading to a big pond — A catfish alongside a gray whale — Useless allegories in a sea of witticisms. What have we learned from our failures? We’ve learned what **not** to do.

Don't Forget the Turtle on the Fence Post

Don't be afraid to ask for help! There is no such thing as a self-made man. If we hear someone say, "**Nobody** has ever helped me, and I'm successful," chances are that person received a great deal of help. The sad thing is that along with success has come conceit. In his arrogance, he is convinced that no one helped him achieve success.

Someone once said, "One thing is for sure, if you see a turtle on top of a fence post, you know he had help getting there." Although, if it's the arrogant, "self-made" man we're talking about, I would modify that statement to read, "One thing is for sure, if you see a *turkey* on top of a fence post, you know he had help getting there."

Believe it or not, there are still people in this world who love to see others achieve success and will do whatever they can to help. We need to be careful when we reach our goal that we don't become full of pride. The closer we get to our God-inspired dreams, the more humble and grateful we should become. And, we should all be helping someone else along the way.

It takes humility to ask for help. However, in seeking godly counsel we *can* avoid making *too many* mistakes. **I hate making mistakes.** Why? Not because I'm full of pride! And, not because I'm afraid someone will see it and then I'll be embarrassed. I've embarrassed myself so many times in my life I'm beginning to enjoy it. I have a wonderful time laughing and making fun of myself.

The reason I hate making mistakes is that it *wastes time*! I enjoy making the most of my day, the most of my week, and the most of my year. So, before I ever make big decisions, I've learned to consult with several people. I listen closely, and many times even take notes.

I've also learned *not* to be so quick to announce, **"God told me to..."** I've talked with some Christians, who, if I begin to question them about their plans they become defensive and completely shut out any counsel by saying, "God told me to!" What they're saying at that point is, "There's no more discussing the matter." What can a person say when someone says, "God told me to?" Who are we to question God's leading in someone's life? Especially when they're very adamant about it.

Even if we believe in our hearts that God told us to do something, it shows great depth of character *and Christian maturity* to remain open to wise counsel. Moreover, if we truly believe that God has told us to do something, then why should we be afraid of *godly* counsel? Is God going to contradict Himself? Is He going to speak one thing to our heart and another to a godly person?

Of course, we have to admit that *it's possible* that we could misinterpret the leading of God, *and* the person we're seeking counsel from could misinterpret the leading of God. After all, we are all human. If we perceive in our hearts that we may have misunderstood God's leading in our lives, then we need to **spend time in prayer seeking God's guidance** to try and discern the direction *He* wants us to take. But, it's for that very reason (that we could misunderstand the leading of God) that we need to remain open to wise counsel. Most of the time I have found that if God has truly told me something, it will be confirmed through the counsel of godly men and women.

It also stands to reason that we need to be careful from whom we receive counsel. Seek out people of godly character who walk in His wisdom. Proverbs 1:5 says, *"A wise man will hear and increase learning, and a man of understanding will attain wise counsel."*

We can't close ourselves off to godly advice. We need to seek it out! It could mean the difference between success and failure. Proverbs 1:7 tells us, *"The fear of the Lord is the beginning of knowledge, but fools despise wisdom and instruction."*

Opportunity Wears Overalls

How do we achieve success? Work! Work! Work! Then, when we're through working for the day, get up the next day and work some more! We simply can't deny the fact that success comes through hard work. Thomas Edison explained it well when he said, "Opportunity is missed by most people because it's dressed in overalls and looks like work." We should also remember that true success never comes overnight. Why do you think people have coined the phrase, "The Road to Success?"

On our road to success, we must *always* keep God first and give God the glory for our successes, and believe in Him for strength to endure and overcome the failures. It's also very important to keep our priorities in order while working to achieve. Success is only an illusion if we've abandoned our relationship with God, family, and friends along the way.

We must identify our goals! Be enthusiastic about our future, and cultivate that enthusiasm with godly friendships and wise counsel. Don't be afraid to ask for help! Always remain humble, grateful, *and teachable*. The truth is, none of us can pursue God's plans on our own. *He never expected us to.*

Lastly, we need to keep this in mind — if we go looking for the easy road we may find it, but in the long run we may be very disappointed. On the other hand, if we enjoy what we're doing, even though it may be difficult, we will find great satisfaction in the midst of hard times. While we work hard pursuing our dreams, we must not forget to enjoy the view along the way.

> ***"EVERY HUMAN MIND IS A GREAT SLUMBERING POWER UNTIL AWAKENED BY A KEEN SPECIFIC DESIRE AND DEFINITE RESOLUTION TO DO."***
>
> ***— Edgar F. Roberts***

Chapter 7

Loose Lips Sink Friendships

Polly, a helpful parishioner, called the church office on Monday to ask the church secretary to be sure the pastor reminds people to bring a covered dish to the potluck on Sunday. The secretary quickly scribbled this announcement — "Pastor, please announce that Polly is in charge of covered dishes on potluck Sunday."

The following day, the associate pastor tried to make sense of the secretary's garbled note. His decoded, unchecked, announcement for the pastor read: "Pastor, announce that Polly will cover the dishes of pot on Sunday."

Shortly before Wednesday night's service, the head usher rapidly perused the prayer request and announcements. Unwittingly, he revised the announcement to read: "Pastor, please announce that Polly will dish out the pot on Sunday."

The congregation became quiet as the pastor paused during his reading of the announcements. Momentarily stunned, he realized there must have been an error in printing the announcements. Then he chuckled as he said, "It seems as though our sister Polly has discovered an unusual way to liven up my sermons!"

Remember playing the telephone game in grade school? The teacher whispers to the first student in the first row, *"The horse ran through the meadow."* Then that student whispers the message to the second. Then the second to the third, and so on. After the message is whispered to the last student the teacher asks, "What's the message?" The last student proudly exclaims, **"Flabby chickens need Hula-Hoops!"** As with the note to the pastor, we see that information filtered through imperfect vessels easily becomes distorted.

The object lesson learned is that when we gossip about others, sooner or later the facts become warped, the truth is twisted, and people can get hurt. Webster's defines "gossip" as idle talk about the affairs of others; go about tattling. It's been said that "the eyes are the windows of the soul." However, when we gossip we unwrap our soul and expose our immaturity. Like someone else once said, "Maybe the eyes are the windows of the soul, but that still doesn't make the mouth the door to the brain."
The question we will pursue is:

Why Do People Gossip?

1. Idleness

In 1 Timothy 5:11-16, Paul talks with Timothy concerning young, unmarried widows. A large part of Paul's concern had to do with idleness. The widows Paul was referring to had too much time on their hands. In verse 13 of chapter 5, Paul says, *"And besides they learn to be idle, wandering about from house to house, and not only idle but also gossips and busybodies, saying things which they ought not."* Paul goes on to imply that their gossipy-busybody ways gave *"opportunity to the adversary* [the devil] *to speak reproachfully."* Then he said, ***"For some have already turned aside after Satan."***

In other words, because they engaged in gossip and because they were busybodies in other people's matters, they opened themselves up to being used as a mouthpiece by the devil so that he could speak reproachfully (blame, discredit, find fault). Also 1 Timothy 5:13 indicates that being a gossip and busybody even caused some to turn away from God. That's a mouthful to chew on!

Who was it that said, "An idle mind is the devil's workshop?" (Get it? Who was it that said…? Hmmm, let me think…) God's Word has much to say about idleness. Proverbs 31:10-31 describes a virtuous wife. In verse 27 of chapter 31, it says, *"She watches over the ways of her household,* ***and does not eat the bread of idleness.****"* Lest you think this chapter is chauvinistic, let me say that men and women can be guilty of "idle talk," and all of us will have to answer to God for idle words that are spoken.

In Matthew 12:24, the Pharisees were slandering Jesus. After Jesus healed a demon-possessed person, the Pharisees accused Jesus of being a devil because he cast out a demon. Consider how warped that theology is! In Matthew 12:25-30, Jesus corrects their theology (demons

101). Then, in verse 33, Jesus talks about how a tree, which in this case represents a person, is known by its *fruit* (words and actions).

We'll pick it up in verse 34 where Jesus calls the Pharisees a *brood of vipers*. ***"Brood of vipers!*** *How can you being evil, speak good things? For out of the abundance of the heart the mouth speaks. A good man out of the treasure of his heart brings forth good things, and an evil man out of the evil treasure brings forth evil things.* ***But I say to you that for every idle word men may speak, they will give account of it in the day of judgment. For by your words you will be justified, and by your words you will be condemned."*** Once again, Jesus cut right to the heart of the matter!

The Pharisees must have had a lot of time on their hands for them to be able to follow Jesus around and slander Him. Again we see, as Paul so brilliantly stated, the Pharisees idleness "gave opportunity to the adversary to speak reproachfully."

We need to keep ourselves from being idle and bored. Idleness can lead to many things, not the least of which are gossip, perverseness, and poverty. In this electronic age we live in with TV *idle* talk shows, sex on the Internet, and telephones that you can take anywhere, the temptations in the midst of idleness are almost more than some folks can bear. We must be *very, very* careful and remember that we will have to answer to God for idle words and actions. Let's stay focused, as Jesus was, and be about the Father's business.

2. Insecurity/Envy

Webster's defines "insecurity" as a lack of assurance or sureness; uncertainty; instability. Interestingly, "envy" is defined as a feeling of discontent or mortification [humiliation], usually with ill will at seeing another person's superior ability, advantages, or success.

The underlying reasons some people feel envious and insecure over someone else's stature or status in life varies from person to person almost as much as personalities. Insecurity in one's life could be the result of not receiving enough attention and reassurance from parents or guardians during crucial formative years.

It could also be the result of a catastrophically embarrassing moment which played havoc with his or her self-esteem. Growing up in abject poverty can induce strong feelings of bitterness toward those who were *"better off."* Volumes of books have been written on such subjects, therefore I will not delve into all of the causes for these conditions.

One of the many wonderful things about the Word of God is that no matter what our reasons for insecurity or envy are, the Bible addresses these issues and leaves us with no excuse. The *cause* for our *"condition"* is of no consequence to God because He not only addresses all of life's issues on an equal plane, but also because His Word provides freedom from **all** sin and bondage. Therefore, there is only one question that remains: will we accept the Word of God as truth over our circumstances, thus putting the Word of God into action in our lives giving us the true freedom we desire? Keep that in mind as you read on.

Insecurity can cause a person to feel as though he must be "in the know." A person who is insecure doesn't want to be left out of "the loop." For that reason, he is forced to keep up with everything that's going on so he can have the "inside track." I'm sure you get the point by now! But, like someone once said, "A gossip burns the scandal at both ends."

Many times an insecure person feels as if he has to please everyone and cannot stand the feeling of not being liked or accepted. What a heavy burden to carry! This of course leads to gossip and backbiting if he's going to please each group. Oh, what a tangled web we weave…!

Gossip that is drawn out of the well of envy and insecurity is some of the most vicious types of gossip. "Did you see the new car John and his wife bought? They just want everyone to see how much money they have! I just can't believe they flaunt their money like that! Did you know John's wife Rita bought herself a new diamond bracelet? You should have seen how she shoved it right in Marcy's face at the grocery store the other day!"

The ironic thing is that the whole time this person gossips about John and Rita, they're wishing *they* were the ones buying the new car and diamond bracelet so *they* could flaunt it just like John and Rita.

Let's face it, everyone — *if* they were truly honest — has envious thoughts now and then. It's one thing to have a thought. It's quite another thing if you allow a wrong thought to take root in your heart. Sooner or later, whatever you've meditated on and allowed to take root in your heart will produce words and actions. Remember what Jesus said in Matthew 12:34? Jesus said, *"Out of the abundance of the heart the mouth speaks."*

Insecurity and envy manifest differently in different people. Probably the most common manifestation is gossip or slander (false statements). Gender also plays a role. Women usually resort to harsh cutting words that can dig deep into a person's soul and cause much pain.

Oftentimes men forgo using words to express their envy or insecurity, and instead act out physically with one another. We even see this in grade school-age boys and girls. Insecurity and envy have even caused men to kill one another. Sadly, in the times we live in, it's even caused young boys and girls to kill each other.

In Genesis 4:8, we see the first murder in the history of mankind. *"Now Cain talked with Abel his brother; and it came to pass, when they were in the field, that Cain rose up against Abel his brother and killed him."* What caused such anger in Cain? Look back in verses 3-5. *"And in the process of time it came to pass that Cain brought an offering of the fruit of the ground to the Lord. Abel also brought of the firstborn of his flock and of their fat. And the Lord respected Abel and his offering,* ***but He did not respect Cain and his offering. And Cain was very angry, and his countenance fell."***

There have been theological debates as to whether it was Cain's offering itself that displeased God, or the attitude in which he presented it to God. Nevertheless, it's obvious that Cain did not feel accepted and you can sense the jealousy born in his heart toward his brother. Bear in mind that God was not being harsh or cruel toward Cain.

Look in verses 6-7. *"So the Lord said to Cain, 'Why are you angry? And why has your countenance fallen? If you do well, will you not be accepted? And if you do not do well, sin lies at the door. And its desire is for you, but you should rule over it.'"*

There is so much we can learn from those two verses of Scripture. If God is omniscient (all knowing), then why did He ask Cain why he was angry? God did the same thing in the Garden of Eden when He called out to Adam and said, "Where are you?" Would you believe earthly fathers do the same thing? Many times when my children are upset I know the reason. Nevertheless, I do the same thing simply because I want them to talk to me about what's bothering them. It's my desire that they *choose* to come and talk with me and share their feelings.

A good father desires open, honest communication with his children that's not initiated through coercive methods. I believe that God's desire was for Cain to come to Him as an act of his will, freely communicating with Him and sharing from his heart. God was simply opening up the lines of communication by initiating the conversation. God *loved* Cain, and He wanted Cain to seek *His help* through repentance. Earthly fathers could glean so much by observing how our heavenly Father deals with His children.

God consoled, instructed, and warned Cain by telling him, "If you do well, will you not be accepted? And if you do not do well, sin lies at the door. And its desire is for you, but you should rule over it." This instruction and warning can apply to any person, anywhere, at any time. To any person who feels insecure; to anyone who feels envious; to any person who feels as if he is about to lash out against friend or foe, **heed this instruction and warning God gave to Cain!** Remember *if we do well, we will be accepted.* If we do not do well, **sin lies at the door. Sin's desire is for us! But it's God's will that we should rule over sin!**

3. Arrogance and Pride

A man brought his boss home for dinner for the first time. The boss was very blustery, arrogant and dominating! The little boy in the family stared at his father's boss for most of the evening, but did not say anything.

Finally, the boss asked the little boy, "Why do you keep looking at me like that, Sonny?"

The little boy answered, "My daddy says you are a self-made man."

The boss beamed and proudly admitted that indeed he was a self-made man.

The little boy said, "Well, if you are a self-made man, why did you make yourself like that?" [10]

Arrogance and pride are very ugly! People in positions of power who are filled with pride and bloated with self-importance can be duped into thinking they are well liked by their subordinates. This happens because people walk on egg shells around them and kowtow to their every whim. It's really a shame because they go through life never being free from their misery simply because no one has the guts to be honest with them. Or when someone they respect finally does address the issue, they may not change because the roots of arrogance and pride have grown too deep.

That same arrogance and pride-filled attitude is what caused the Pharisees to slander Jesus. The *Pharisees* were a sect of the Jews who believed in strict interpretation of the Law of Moses. When Jesus came to the earth and began to teach the truth it was a direct assault on the self-made, self righteousness of the Pharisees. The Pharisees had influence and power as religious leaders, and were obviously threatened by the truth Jesus taught which He proclaimed "would make you free." (See John 8:32.)

People do the same thing today. Say we have a circle of friends and someone new joins our circle. If we have someone in our circle who is somewhat arrogant or filled with pride, we may notice a change in that person. This will be magnified even more if the new kid on the block has any type of charismatic qualities. Suddenly, the arrogant one, who probably enjoys most of the attention and control, feels threatened by the charismatic newcomer.

---

[10] *Sunday Sermons,* November-December 1987.

Just as envy and insecurity will cause this reaction, so will arrogance and pride. The difference is that people who are full of pride, many times will allow deep bitterness and anger to fill their hearts. Then they become hurt, but are too proud to admit it.

When a person who is full of pride and arrogance gets hurt by people, he can easily separate himself from people. His overactive pride tells him he doesn't need anyone. He can make it on his own! Self-righteousness assures him that he is right, and everyone else is wrong! Then, he not only gossips, but he also becomes an insufferable critic of everyone else's lives.

Humility is a choice just like anything else we do in life. Proverbs 16:5 says, *"Everyone proud in heart is an abomination to the Lord;* ***though they join forces, none will go unpunished.****"* And, Proverbs 6:16-19 very clearly tells us how God feels concerning pride and gossip: *"These six things the Lord hates, yes, seven are an abomination to Him:* ***A proud look, a lying tongue,*** *hands that shed innocent blood, a heart that devises wicked plans, feet that are swift in running to evil,* ***a false witness who speaks lies, and one who sows discord among brethren."***

When we understand God's thoughts concerning pride and arrogance, if we desire to be pleasing to Him, we will choose to live a life of humility toward God and toward man.

4. Untrustworthy

Let's face it, there are simply some people who can't be trusted. They love to tell the story. Unfortunately, not the story of "unseen things above." They love to be in the know so they can blow. Have you ever known people like this? You almost feel sorry for them because they can't keep their mouths shut!

Alan Herbert once said, "If no one ever spoke unless he knew what he was talking about, a ghastly hush would descend upon the earth." The Bible has a lot to say about being trustworthy, and not being a "talebearer." Proverbs 11:13 says, *"A talebearer reveals secrets, but he who is of a faithful spirit conceals a matter."*

Trust is something that is earned. What happens when you lose trust in someone? What do we do when our sixteen-year-old, who has a driver's license hot off the press, tells us he's going to the movies with a friend and we find out later he spent the evening somewhere he shouldn't have been? Now he's not only lost our trust, but more than likely the privilege of driving the car for awhile. When does he get it back? When we feel as though he's earned our trust.

Aren't adults the same way? Don't we seek friendships with those to whom we feel we can bare our souls? Don't we value friends we feel confident can "conceal a matter"? True friendships rest upon openness, honesty, and trust. Proverbs 27:6 says, *"Faithful are the wounds of a friend, but the kisses of an enemy are deceitful."*

> *And the sweetness of man's friend gives delight by hearty counsel.*
>
> *Proverbs 27:9*

> *Do not forsake your own friend or your father's friend.*
>
> *Proverbs 27:10*

We all need a friend we can trust and with whom we can be totally transparent. But, who wants to be friends with someone who is an untrustworthy gossip? We'll never feel comfortable enough to open up and be completely honest because we're afraid of who might find out the secrets of our heart. Be a friend who has a faithful spirit and conceals a matter.

I realize that *on occasion* we must talk about the affairs of others. For example, a supervisor calls us in the office because he thinks Joe Slinky is taking money out of the coffee fund. Job evaluations are another time when people are talked about.

Nevertheless, we must learn to recognize in our consciences where to draw the line between *concern* and *gossip*. Sometimes we try to conceal gossip by using the phrase, "I'm *concerned* about So-and-So." If we're that concerned then why don't we go speak to So-and-So? Or, pray for So-and-So?

As a man once said, "We need to live our lives so that we wouldn't be ashamed to sell our family parrot to the town gossip." Christians should not be known for gossip. We should be known for being trustworthy people who can control our mouths. Take to heart what James 1:26 says, *"If anyone among you thinks he is religious, and does not bridle his tongue but deceives his own heart,* ***this one's religion is useless****."* Don't deceive your own heart!

Finally, James 3:2 tells us, *"For we all stumble in many things. If anyone does not stumble in word, he is a perfect* [mature] *man,* ***able also to bridle the whole body****."* Wow! Now there's a goal to shoot for! We need to ask ourselves, "How many people do I know like that?" Then, ask a more important question, "Am **I** like that?"

WE MUST BE PEOPLE OF GODLY CHARACTER IF WE ARE GOING TO HAVE AN IMPACT ON THE WORLD AROUND US.

Chapter 8

Reduced to a Crust of Bread

The CEO of a large corporation was asked at a Weight Watchers meeting how he had become so grossly overweight. The CEO answered, "Everyday I encounter a large amount of stress because I am continually called upon to make decisions of great magnitude."

The leader of the Weight Watchers meeting inquired, "So stress has caused you to overeat?"

"No" the CEO replied, "I never make big decisions on an empty stomach!"

I'm a people watcher. I'm the kind of person who could get enjoyment out of sitting on a bench in a busy shopping mall, *with a large Dr. Pepper*, just observing people. I am greatly intrigued by people and their actions.

As I sit and observe, I wonder, "*Why did that person go into that store? Why did that person choose to get a snake tattoo on the neck and a silver studded earring in the tongue?*" As I'm writing this I'm wondering what type of person might be reading this? Why did you choose this book and what impact will it have in your life?

Just think, right at this very moment there are literally billions of people in this world who are making a choice of one kind or another. They could be making a very non-threatening choice like what to have for dinner. It's very likely that at this moment someone, somewhere, is making a choice concerning whether to cheat on a spouse. And, somewhere there is an innocent party of marital infidelity who might be considering divorce.

It's also possible that somewhere in the world someone is considering taking his own life, while thousands of other people are contemplating doing something nice for someone. Isn't it fascinating that at any given moment in this world there are an innumerable score of decisions being made for better or for worse! Every moment of the day the world is a gigantic collage of people making choices.

Wow, Jeff, this is getting too deep for me! Well, just imagine what God has to deal with! **Thank God we are not God!** Although, all this thinking (even though it tweaks my brain) does cause me to evaluate my own life and the choices I make on a daily basis. Are they godly choices? How do my decisions affect the lives of others? As Christians, we're not in this thing to satisfy ourselves. We are commissioned by God to live a life that's pleasing to Him, and that has a loving impact on others.

Proverbs 6:26 says, *"For by means of a harlot a man is reduced to a crust of bread."* That verse speaks of more than just a man who sleeps with a prostitute. We all make decisions on a daily basis concerning the things we will pursue in life. We can choose to pursue spiritual things, or worldly things. The choices we make can lead to great blessings, mediocrity, or poverty and shame. If we choose to follow the teaching of the Word of God it will lead to a peaceful and successful life. Let's look at a few topics relating to the choices we make.

What Catches Your Heart?

Tim Redmond said, "There are many things that will catch my eye, but there are only a few that catch my heart. It is those things I consider to pursue." What catches your heart? What things do you consider to pursue? Our flesh, our human nature, our unregenerate souls, seem to constantly get in the way of a fruitful walk with God. **Does it have to be that way?** I don't think so!

Men have to be extremely careful about what *catches their eyes*, while women have to be very sensitive to what they allow to *catch their hearts*. Men are very visual in nature. God created men that way. So, with men something usually catches the eye first, and then it goes to the heart.

Women, on the other hand, tend to be much more sensitive emotionally. God created women that way. With women, many times it's not so much the visual effect of something, but the emotional effect. An exception is the woman who said she only needs four men in her life: a banker, an actor, a minister, and a mortician. One for the money, two for the show, three to get ready, and four to go! [11]

---

[11] *Parables Etc.,* June 1983, submitted by Charles Kinyon

In Matthew 5:28, Jesus said, *"But I say to you that whoever looks at a woman to lust for her has already committed adultery with her in his heart."* Notice it begins by looking, and then allowing what our eyes have focused on to produce thoughts that take root in our hearts.

> *For though we walk in the flesh, we do not war according to the flesh.*
>
> *For the weapons of our warfare are not carnal but mighty in God for pulling down strongholds,*
>
> *Casting down arguments* ***and every high thing that exalts itself against the knowledge of God, bringing every thought into captivity to the obedience of Christ.***
>
> *2 Corinthians 10:3-5*

There are several things that jump out at me in that piece of scripture.

1. To truly exercise authority over strongholds we must stay built up in the Lord. Why? Because, it says the weapons of our warfare are mighty IN GOD *for pulling down strongholds*. We can't live as the world lives and expect to have victory over strongholds in our life.

2. Strongholds are mentioned with arguments *and every high thing that exalts itself against the knowledge of God.* We must know the Word of God s*o we can recognize arguments* that are exalting themselves against the knowledge of God. That was one of Eve's problems. She didn't listen to God's instructions closely enough to be able to judge whether the devil was telling her the truth, or whether he was feeding her a lie.

3. It's up to *us* to bring every thought into captivity *to the obedience of Christ*. Jesus said, "Whoever looks at a woman to *lust for her…*" It's one thing for a man to look at a woman. It's another for him to look at her to lust for her. When he begins to lust for her, he has gone beyond a glance. What he has seen with his eyes has now become a meditation of his heart. That's why Proverbs 4:23 says, *"Keep your heart with all diligence, for out of it spring the issues of life."*

Bringing thoughts into captivity — *to the obedience of Christ* — means we're thinking about what we're thinking about. In other words, we judge our thoughts according to the Word of God, and reject those thoughts that aren't befitting an ambassador of Christ.

Proverbs 4 goes on to say, *"Put away from you a deceitful mouth, and put perverse lips far from you. Let your eyes look straight ahead, and your eyelids look right before you.* ***Ponder the path of your feet, and let all your ways be established. Do not turn to the right or the left; remove your foot from evil."***

Just as we can *choose* to allow our eyes to focus on *ungodly things*, we can also *choose* to envision and meditate on godly things. Psalm 19:14 says, *"Let the words of my mouth and the meditation of my heart be acceptable in Your sight, O Lord, my strength and my Redeemer."*

Rarely, if ever, do we come across an actual situation where someone's arm was twisted, and they were *forced* to engage in a sinful act. Or, as Flip Wilson's character Geraldine used to say, *"The devil made me do it!"* It's possible to meditate on good things every day. Is it easy all the time? No. Nevertheless, by the power and strength of the Spirit of God within us, we can exercise self-control and reject those thoughts that try to exalt themselves against the knowledge of God.

The apostle Paul explains to the Philippians the best way to combat any thoughts the devil may throw your way. In Philippians 4:8-9, it says, *"Finally, brethren, whatever things are true, whatever things are noble, whatever things are just, whatever things are pure, whatever things are lovely, whatever things are of good report, if there is any virtue and if there is anything praiseworthy —* ***meditate on these things****. The things which you learned and received and heard and saw in me,* ***these do, and the God of peace will be with you."***

Don't Throw Away Your Inheritance!

> *Two nations are in your womb, two peoples shall be separated from your body; one people shall be stronger than the other, and the older shall serve the younger.*
>
> *Genesis 25:23*

Those were the words the Lord spoke to Rebekah when she was pregnant with Esau and Jacob. Rebekah gave birth to twins just as the Lord prophesied. Verses 25-28 say, *"And the first came out red. He was like a hairy garment all over; so they called his name Esau. Afterward his brother came out and his hand took hold of Esau's heel; so his name was called Jacob. Isaac* [their father — Abraham's son] *was sixty years old when she bore them. So the boys grew. And Esau was a skillful hunter, a man of the field; but Jacob was a mild man, dwelling in tents. And Isaac loved Esau because he ate of his game, but Rebekah loved Jacob."*

That's a quick background of the story of Esau and Jacob. Jacob's name meant supplanter, or deceitful, literally one who takes the heel. Guess what Esau's name meant — you guessed it — *hairy*. Boy, just imagine being a toddler and getting a Norelco electric razor for Christmas! Rebekah favored Jacob and Isaac favored Esau. Esau, being the firstborn, was entitled to the birthright which meant headship of the family and a double inheritance (See Deuteronomy 21:17.)

Now we continue the hairy deceitful saga. Genesis 25:29-34 says, *"Now Jacob cooked a stew; and Esau came in from the field, and he was weary. And Esau said to Jacob, 'Please feed me with that same red stew, for I am weary.' Therefore his name was called Edom. But Jacob said, 'Sell me your birthright as of this day.' And Esau said, 'Look, I am about to die;* ***so what is this birthright to me****?' Then Jacob said, 'Swear to me as of this day.' So he swore to him, and sold his birthright to Jacob. And Jacob gave Esau bread and stew of lentils; then he ate and drank, arose, and went his way. Thus Esau despised his birthright."* (Note: Edom means red.)

Let's consider what Esau was in line to inherit. Isaac (Esau's father) had inherited everything his father Abraham possessed. (See Genesis 25:5.) Because Abraham was faithful to God and obeyed Him, God made Abraham very, very rich. Therefore, Isaac inherited a great amount of wealth.

Isaac became even wealthier than his father Abraham. In Genesis 26: 12-13 it says, *"Then Isaac sowed in that land, and reaped in the same year a hundredfold; and the Lord blessed him. The man began to prosper, and continued prospering until he became very prosperous."* I would love to prosper, and continue prospering until I became very prosperous. That scripture seems humorously redundant, but I think you get the point. Isaac was wealthy!

So Esau comes in from the field *about to die*! Oh really? Do you think Esau may have been a little overly dramatic? Anyway, Jacob is cooking up a red stew (maybe the first Cajun stew?). Esau wants some stew, and Jacob responds the way any of us might, *"Sell me your birthright as of this day."*

Esau **should have** fallen on the floor laughing and saying, "Let me get this straight. You want all of my unspeakable wealth for some red stew? **I** don't think so!" But instead Esau sold his birthright to Jacob for bread and stew of lentils. Which, by the way, was legal according to Hurrian custom. So the Bible says Esau *despised* his birthright.

Esau's grievously misguided benevolence even gained him a spot in New Testament writings. In Hebrews 12:16-17 it says, *"Lest there be any fornicator or profane* [godless] *person like Esau, who for one morsel of food sold his birthright. For you know that afterward, when he wanted to inherit a blessing, he was rejected, for he found no place for repentance, though he sought it diligently with tears."* That's a pretty dismal legacy, and a very solemn warning!

When a person, such as Esau, is driven by lust for things (whether it be sex, food, or material wealth) it not only diminishes him in moral character, but it tears away at the fiber of his entire life. Notice in Hebrews 12:17 it says, *"Esau found no place for repentance, though he sought it diligently with tears."* Esau gave away the most precious thing his father could give him in exchange for immediate fleshly gratification.

Many Christians have given away their inheritance in order to satisfy their flesh. It's a very grave thing in the sight of God for one of His children to give away his inheritance!

Take into account these words in Hebrews 10:26-31: *"For if we sin willfully after we have received the knowledge of the truth, there no longer remains a sacrifice for sins, but a certain fearful expectation of judgment, and fiery indignation which will devour the adversaries. Anyone who has rejected Moses' law dies without mercy (speaking of those who lived under Old Testament Law) on the testimony of two or three witnesses. Of how much worse punishment, do you suppose, will he be thought worthy who has trampled the Son of God underfoot,* ***counted the blood of the covenant by which he was sanctified a common thing, and insulted the Spirit of grace?*** *For we know Him who said, 'Vengeance is Mine, I will repay,' says the Lord. And again, 'The Lord will judge His people.'* ***It is a fearful thing to fall into the hands of the living God."***

One who "sins willfully," so that there *no longer remains a sacrifice for sins*, is obviously not a person who is trying to serve God but commits an act of sin. If that were true, none of us would be able to seek forgiveness from the Father who is, "faithful and just to forgive us our sins and to cleanse us from all unrighteousness." If that were true, the prodigal son would not have been able to return to the Father's house after *willfully* squandering his inheritance.

It's clearly a reference to a person like Esau who not only understood that he possessed an inheritance, *but who willingly gave up that inheritance* as if it were *a common thing* to be tossed out like trash. In other words, the behavior of the prodigal son appears to be rooted in immaturity. In contrast, it seems as though Esau *understood* his inheritance, yet he *despised* it! Esau sold his inheritance to *satisfy his flesh.*

Obviously, the prodigal son is more representative of an immature Christian who doesn't fully understand the *value of his inheritance.* Even though the prodigal son understood *he had* an inheritance, *he made an impetuous decision to take it*, and then acted foolishly with it like a child who doesn't comprehend it's worth. And, unlike Esau, the prodigal son *found repentance* and was welcomed back to the Father's house.

The bottom line is this: Our godly inheritance, as a child of the Almighty, is *too valuable and precious to play around with.* Not to mention the unimaginable sacrifice God made to procure our salvation. **The blood of the covenant is not a common thing!** We should make up our minds to live a life of honor before the Father. We should *never* insult the Spirit of Grace by turning our back on the Lord and tossing away our inheritance as if it were a piece of garbage. We need to thank God for our inheritance! Let us always remain faithful and loyal to the One who has provided it for us!

Where Do You Find Peace?

I heard a true story of a retired couple who were frightened by the threat of nuclear war. They began a serious study to find the safest place on the earth. They studied and traveled, traveled and studied. Finally, they found THE PLACE. On Christmas they sent their pastor a card from their new home — in the Falkland Islands — *just prior to the war between Argentina and Great Britain.*

In John 14:27, Jesus said, *"Peace I leave with you, My peace I give to you; not as the world gives do I give to you. Let not your heart be troubled, neither let it be afraid."* Jesus says very clearly that there is a tremendous difference between the peace He gives versus the world's version of peace.

How do people in the world try to find peace? Maybe through a psychiatrist? Possibly through alcohol or drugs. Some try to find peace through psychics or false religions. Maybe we could achieve *world peace* if everyone in the world would hold hands while standing barefoot and chanting the William Tell Overture with popsicles between their toes on the night of a full moon!

Frankly, I'm surprised no one has thought of that yet. It seems perfectly logical to me! Being barefoot represents openness and honesty with our fellow humans. The William Tell Overture represents the common thread of music which binds the souls of all creatures. Chanting, *as we all know,* energizes a harmonic convergence of all the minds in the universe. Of course, the popsicles between the toes during a full moon needs no explanation!

Does that sound ridiculous to you? (I would hope that it does.) Sometimes it boggles the mind what people try to conjure up in their pursuit of peace. And, interestingly enough, my wife just interrupted my writing to tell me of a story she just saw on the news concerning a man in Japan whose wife committed suicide over a decade ago.

Apparently, his family would not give their blessing to his first marriage and they never accepted the union. The man and his family wanted to make amends so that his late wife's soul could rest in peace. So, what does the man do? He marries a Barbie doll! (seems logical to me!) On the news, they showed a picture of him exiting the ceremony with the doll! Now his family could bless the union thereby allowing his late wife to rest in peace. (That certainly makes my world peace idea look dull!)

The way to find peace is really very simple. Isaiah 26:3 says, *"You will keep him in perfect peace* ***whose mind is stayed on You. Because he trusts in You."*** Why do so many people look for peace everywhere except the Bible? As with the man in Japan, it could be the result of strange religious practices or corrupt Bible doctrine.

The rhetorical question I would like to ask is this: Why do so many people, when presented with *sound biblical answers*, choose to seek *unbiblical* ways to find peace? I believe the major reason is that serving God requires *time, commitment*, and *obedience* to His Word! Our fast-paced culture does very little to cultivate commitment in people's lives. People either don't make the time, or they want a *free ride* — no effort involved.

Notice how Isaiah said God will keep those in perfect peace *whose mind is stayed on Him?* Keeping our thoughts on God requires some effort. Knowing God's Word and spending time with Him requires commitment. **Christians have to begin to pray against apathy in the local church.** The pull of the world through entertainment and so many things **that satisfy self** is *very, very* strong. So many people desire peace in their life, yet they're not willing to get up and go to church, or spend time with God on their own.

There is no secret formula to having peace in our hearts. Peace is very easy to find, although it does require some effort on our part. *We* have to *keep our minds on Him, and trust in Him.* We will have trials pop up as we pursue God. Remember that even in the midst of the trials we can have peace in our heart. But, once again, *it is our choice.*

Have Your Cake and Eat It Too

So many people in the world today want to have their cake and eat it too. They want to be able to live selfish lifestyles, ignoring the principles of the Word of God, *and then* have eternal life with the Father when their lives are over.

What they don't understand is that with God we *can* have our cake and eat it too, **but not the worldly way**. God's cake is a different kind of cake. It's not full of worldly ideas and lusts of the flesh. The food that I'm talking about is spiritual food that *satisfies the soul*. With God, we *can* enjoy life to it's fullest, *then afterward* spend eternity with Him. The best part is, we won't spend half our life with our face in a porcelain suction hole because we had *"one too many."*

A life spent pursuing worldly things that only satisfy the flesh will become very dull after awhile. Plus, a person who lives his whole life pursuing fleshly satisfaction will end up as Proverbs 6:26 says, *"...reduced to a crust of bread."* Why? Because things of this earth have a strange way of rusting, deteriorating, and falling apart. Even our physical body goes back to the dust from where it came.

Proverbs 23:4-5 says, ***"Do not overwork to be rich;*** *because of your own understanding, cease! Will you set your eyes on that which is not?* ***For riches certainly make themselves wings; they fly away like an eagle toward heaven."*** Wealth has a funny way of taking wings and disappearing. We can't trust in riches. We need to put our trust in God!

In Matthew 6:19, Jesus said, *"**Do not** lay up for yourselves treasures on earth, where moth and rust destroy and where thieves break in and steal;* ***but lay up for yourselves treasures in heaven,*** *where neither moth nor* *rust destroys and where thieves do not break in and steal.* ***For where your treasure is, there your heart will be also."***

What do we treasure the most in life? Do we treasure worldly things, or do we treasure God's Word and His presence? Like anything else in life, it's our choice, and no one else can make it for us.

We need to choose the godly kind of life! We should enjoy our inheritance as children of God, and not strive to keep up with the Joneses. We can enjoy the peace of God in our lives as we delight in His Word and abide in His presence, and store up treasures in heaven by obeying God and living a life that makes Him proud to call us His child.

WE CAN CHOOSE GOD'S WAY EVERYDAY. WE CAN CHOOSE PEACE, JOY, AND STRENGTH IN THE HOLY GHOST! WE CAN EVEN CHOOSE GODLY PROSPERITY WITHOUT THE NOTION OF HAVING TO KEEP UP WITH THE JONESES.

Chapter 9

Who Are the Joneses Anyway?

The New Modern Math

Teaching Math in 1950: *A logger sells a truckload of lumber for $100. His cost of production is 4/5 of the price. What is his profit?*

Teaching Math in 1960: *A logger sells a truckload of lumber for $100. His cost of production is 4/5 of the price, or $80. What is his profit?*

Teaching Math in 1970: *A logger exchanges a set "L" of lumber for a set "M" of money. The carnality of set "M" is 100. Each element is worth one dollar. Make 100 dots representing the elements of the set "M". The set "C", the cost of production, contains 20 fewer points than set "M". Represent the set "C" as a subset of* *set "M" and answer the following question: What is the carnality of the set "P" for profits?*

Teaching Math in 1980: *A logger sells a truckload of lumber for $100. Her cost of production is $80. And her profit is $20. Your assignment: Underline the number 20.*

Teaching Math in 1990: *By cutting down beautiful forest trees, the logger makes $20. What do you think of this way of making a living? Topic for class participation after answering the question: How did the forest birds and squirrels feel as the logger cut down the trees? There are no wrong answers.*

Teaching Math in 1996: *By laying off 40% of its loggers, a company improves its stock price from $80 to $100. How much capital gain per share does the CEO make by exercising his stock options at $80? Assume capital gains are no longer taxed, because this encourages investment.*

Teaching Math in 1997: *A company outsources all of its loggers. The firm saves on benefits, and when demand for its product is down, the logging work force can easily be cut back. The average logger employed by the company earned $50,000, had three weeks vacation, a nice retirement plan and medical insurance. The contracted logger charges $50 an hour. Was outsourcing loggers a good move for the company?*

Teaching Math in 1999: *A laid off logger serving time in Folsom for blowing away several people was being trained as a COBOL programmer in order to work on the Y2K* *projects. What was the probability that the automatic cell doors would have opened on their own as of 00.00.01, 01/01/00?* [12]

Times have certainly changed! So has the cost of living! My parents' generation (people who grew up in the 40s and 50s) worked hard and made sacrifices in order to acquire the things they have. Their parents lived through the great depression and had learned the value of not accumulating debt (as if they had a choice), and putting something away for a rainy day.

Typically, the younger generation wants everything their parents have as soon as, or shortly after they get married. They forget, of course, that it took their parents years and years of hard work to acquire and to maintain what they own. They want everything now, and many times they'll get it no matter what kind of financial strain it puts on them. Financial pressure is one of the leading causes of marital stress and marital breakups. Is it really worth it?

I don't believe that God wants us to be poor and always in financial pain. The apostle John wrote, *"I pray that you may prosper in all things and be in health,* ***just as your soul prospers****."* (3 John 2) Can we be prosperous and also have a healthy relationship with God? I believe the answer to that question is contingent upon whether or not our souls continually follow *hard after God.* (See Psalm 63:8.)

However, if our highest priority is money and material possessions, it will not only affect our relationship with family and friends, but most importantly, it will affect

---

[12] *The New Modern Math,* by Bruce Laird

our relationship with God. Jesus Himself told us that, *"No servant can serve two masters; for either he will hate the one and love the other, or else he will be loyal to the one and despise the other.* ***You cannot serve God and mammon*** **[riches]***"* (Luke 16:13).

Plush Grass or Artificial Turf?

A church in Houston, Texas, had this phrase on their sign outside their church: "The meek shall inherit the earth." Underneath it, a graffitist had scrawled: "But not the mineral rights." [13] (Only in Texas!)

When I was a police officer, I obviously dealt with people from all walks of life. One of the many things I observed was that people who have a substantial amount of wealth also have problems. And, the solutions to their problems generally cost a lot more money. For example, putting a dent in my Ford mini van is not quite the same as putting a dent in a Jaguar or Rolls Royce. Along with increased wealth and more expensive material possessions, come more problems and higher maintenance cost. Yet, isn't it interesting that those who don't have wealth *think* that if they were *wealthy* they wouldn't have any problems?

Why does the grass always look greener on the other side? Sometimes if we could catch a glimpse of the other side, we may discover that the plush looking grass is nothing but artificial turf.

There are many people in our society who have the appearance of wealth, but when we look underneath, we discover that their houses are mortgaged up to the dimple in their chin and they're on the brink of bankruptcy. Even

---

[13] *Parables Etc.,* May 1985.

so, many people convince themselves that if they could just win the lottery they would be happy. Why? Where does this idea come from?

There's no denying the fact that much of the KUWTJ syndrome begins to develop from the time we are very young. There can be many influences in our lives that play a role. Growing up in poverty can have this effect. If a person grows up having very little, envying those who are "better off," he may spend the rest of his life pursuing material possessions.

The attitudes our parents display will also play a major role: what we *hear* being taught us, and most importantly, *what we see lived before our eyes*. The ideals that our parents display, plus the influence of our peers, help shape our future.

In today's society, sports figures *and* the entertainment industry also play a major role in shaping the attitudes of young people. Many times a young person's perception of what is important in life is formed and polished by what is seen on the Silver Screen.

So often, *parents* **knowingly** play a major role in promoting the idea that we have to keep up materialistically with everyone else. I'm speaking of parents who can't fathom the idea that their child might be thought of as being "uncool," or rejected by their peers because they're not *in style*. As a result, they have to buy them the most hip, up-to-date clothes so they can "fit in" with their peers. Subsequently, their children not only become keenly aware that they must keep up with everyone materially (and feel insecure if they don't), but also they begin to equate love with *things*.

The truly sad thing is, a child should feel *most secure* at home. When parents care more about whether or not their child is accepted by his peers, it's a good indication that they are neglecting their parental responsibility to provide a home environment where their child feels loved and accepted.

It's much easier for parents, especially if both work and hardly ever see their children, to relegate to their children's peers character building and the forming of ideals in their child. These parents comfort themselves by thinking, *"It's OK as long as they're not getting in any real trouble — they're all really pretty good kids."*

Our work environment can also foster the attitude that we must keep up with everyone else. I worked in the secular workplace for many years and I've felt that pressure to KUWTJ. We view our co-workers' affluent lifestyles, and then we sense that pressure to be accepted. What we don't realize is that in order to live that lifestyle, both husband *and* wife have to work to pay for their brand-new SUV and their beautiful new home in an upper middle class neighborhood. Then, on top of that, they max out their credit cards so they can have newest styles for them *and* their children.

When my wife and I got married, I was working as a police officer. We prayed and believed that my wife could stay home when our first child was born. It has always been very important to both of us to pour our lives into our children. Raising children in "the nurture and admonition of the Lord" is a **scriptural mandate** *that you only have one opportunity to accomplish.* We felt the same way when we made the decision to home-school our children.

That meant, however, that we had to live on a single income. We bought an older home (very old, and only 1000 square feet), which needed *a lot of repair.* I'll never forget one night at work, a co-worker of mine mistakenly thought we had purchased a house in a neighborhood that had much nicer homes. I said, "No, that wasn't me." He said, "Oh, *I thought you got yourself a real house."*

We all make *individual* choices concerning our priorities in life. Through police work and being in the ministry, I have seen the problems that wealth and the pursuit of material things can cause. Husband and wife both working long hours just to pay their bills so they can have the newest *stuff.* At the same time they neglect spending time with each other and their children.

They also never find the time to teach their children godly principles, and because they're so busy, many times they neglect getting involved in their local church. The amazing part is, they look absolutely stunned when their child gets in high school and turns his back on biblical morality.

Are the opinions of others causing us to abandon God in order to pursue material possessions so we can "fit in?" Who are the people we're listening to? Remember, Jesus said you can't serve both God and riches. So before we go pursuing all the material things of the world, consider what the end result will be. We need to ask ourselves, *"Is all this stuff more important than my relationship with God, and my relationship with my family?"* The real question is: *Are we trying to please God, or people?*

Diligent Hands Bring Wealth

I don't believe that the Bible teaches we must live in poverty. I believe God wants his people to be prosperous for several very important reasons:

1. So that our families needs can be met;

2. So that we can further God's work; and

3. So that we can be a great blessing to others.

I do believe the scriptures concerning tithing, giving offerings, and sowing and reaping. My wife and I put them into practice in our lives. I'm still relatively young, nevertheless I believe the words of David when he said, *"I've been young, and now am old; yet I have not seen the righteous forsaken, nor his descendants begging bread"* (Psalm 37:25).

I've said all that to say this: now that you know I believe in the scriptural principles concerning God's financial plan, can I discuss the *practical* side of earning money for just a moment *without* being accused of being in doubt and unbelief?

How does the average person make enough money to support a family? In our society there are many different ways to make, or have money. We can inherit money. Yet, let's face it, people inheriting large sums of money is rare. Many people hope to cash in on the Power Ball Lottery, using their high school football number, plus their shoe size, and their wife's birth date backwards. Of course, they disregard the odds of winning the lottery **or the addictive effect it can produce in people's lives**.

How about this: We could be one of the chosen few who breaks into the world of Hollywood with no formal training or education, and makes it big while setting aside all our Christian morals and upbringing so we can become a star. Once again, this is not the norm for the millions and millions of working class people simply trying to make a living nor is it healthy for our spiritual walk.

How does the average Joe make money — legally? The old-fashioned way — *he earns it!* Now think of all the factors involved in earning money. Generally speaking, in our society, higher education equals higher salaries. And, higher education in certain disciplines (medicine, rocket science) opens the door to larger earning potential in the job market.

So when we speak of education we have to factor in giftings and abilities. For instance, I have to face the fact that I will never work in the field of medicine, engineering, rocket science, *or anything involving math.* You wouldn't have to interview many of my close friends or relatives to discover that I show no signs of having any ability in the area of math or science.

When I was in high school, my best subjects were physical education and band. I nearly failed algebra, but I can knock out a mean beat on a set of drums. I love the Word of God and I love people. I can preach three times a week, counsel daily, work on a book, and not think anything of it. But my wife has to balance the checkbook.

With that in mind, there are many people on this earth who, *more than likely,* may never start out earning enormous sums of money using their *natural God-given abilities.* Support their family? Absolutely! I believe God will bless the work of your hands and increase your possessions. (See Job 1:10.) Especially, if you do as Colossians 3:22 says, *"...obey in all things your masters according to the flesh, not with eyeservice, as men-pleasers, but in sincerity of heart,* ***fearing God****."* In other words, work as if God Himself is your boss. Will you become rich? Maybe. Maybe not.

Think of all the wealthy Christians you know personally. How do you think *the majority* of those Christians became wealthy? Did they suddenly have this enormous amount of wealth dropped in their laps? Probably not. More than likely their prosperity is the result of faith, obedience to God, *and hard work.* They put to use the gifts, abilities, and callings that God had placed in them and followed God's leading in their lives. You'll also discover that, more than likely, their prosperity did not come overnight. Generally speaking, biblical prosperity comes from years and years of putting godly principles into practice in our lives.

I have a real problem with Christians who are sitting on their backsides waiting for some miraculous transfer of wealth from the wicked into their pockets. They wait around, while quoting the second half of Proverbs 13:22 which says, *"But the wealth of the sinner is stored up for the righteous,"* hoping someday for a *manifestation.*

If we read the word we'll see how the fulfillment of that scripture has been taking place since the beginning of time. What did God instruct Joshua to do when he went into the Promised Land and defeated his enemies? **They took the enemies' stuff!** The whole nation of Israel prospered when they *obeyed* the Word of God by going out and battling with the enemy and defeating the adversary.

Now, let's bring that scenario into the church age. As New Testament Christians, we understand that the battles which were fought *in the flesh in the Old Testament* were foreshadowings, or representative of, the *spiritual battles* we fight *under the New Covenant.* We don't go out as a church and fight with the unbelievers and take their stuff. That wouldn't look good!

We acquire prosperity by:

1. Exercising our faith, believing that God will bless our **obedience to His Word** (tithing, giving offerings, sowing seed, etc.)
2. Believing God will bless **the work of our hands**
3. Most importantly, through **walking in love!**

Those three principles are the way we acquire anything spiritually. We must believe in our hearts (that God will do what His Word says), put words and actions with our belief (faith without works is dead), and do it *while walking in love* (which exhibits our true underlying motives).

We also have the spiritual authority to stand against the enemy (the devil) who would love to try to stop the flow of the blessings of God in our lives. Even when we resist the devil we must **first** *submit ourselves to God.* (See James 4:7.)

What about the wealth of the wicked being transferred to the righteous? Some believed that the Y2K problem was going to cause great wealth to be transferred to their bank accounts. If that actually did happen to you, let me warn you that there are going to be a couple of people who will come looking for you. The IRS is going to want to know *where you got the money.* And, if it was a *bank error* in your favor, after the bank discovers the error they're going to want *their money back.* Taking money that doesn't belong to us **is not** part of God's plan to prosper us.

Still, if we listen to some Christians talk about this "transfer of wealth" it almost sounds as though they have great animosity toward unbelievers who are wealthy. In their mind they think, *"Those unbelievers have my stuff!"* To me, that doesn't sound like *walking in love*! We have a holy calling in this age of grace to *go into all the world and preach the gospel.* **The gospel we preach is a gospel of peace.** It is the good news concerning God's love toward man, and salvation through His Son.

Boy, we had better check our motives! **God loved the whole world *so much* He gave His only Son!** Shouldn't we have the same love as our Father has for the souls of unbelievers? *Even wealthy unbelievers?* As people of God, we need to get our eyes off the wealth of the unsaved and begin praying for *their souls*!

It's not the unbelievers who are keeping us from prospering. *They are not our enemies!* 2 Corinthians 10:3 says, *"For though we walk in the flesh,* ***we do not war according to the flesh.****"* This is a *spiritual* battle we're in! God requires that we obtain prosperity in these times we're living in *the same as He did in biblical times* — BY FAITH! (See Hebrews 11.)

I have another question: how can God bless the Church (worldwide) the way He wants to when only a small percentage of the Church (as a whole) give their tithes? I realize that there are Christians in individual churches who are obedient to the Word of God, and they are being blessed. In contrast, imagine what the Church worldwide could accomplish if we had 100 percent participation in tithing, and giving offerings above and beyond the tithe! Christians everywhere would be blessed and evangelism would be at an all-time high! Every church would be debt free! We would also be able to fund huge missionary campaigns all over the world!

It seems as though we need to hear less talk about this great transfer of wealth from the wicked, and more uncompromised teaching concerning obedience to God's Word and reaching out to the lost. **Shouldn't we allow judgment to begin with the house of God?**

We must put our faith in God! God wants to prosper us by *His hand.* It will take diligence in pursuing God's plan for our life and obedience to God's principles. We need to pray that God will show us ways to prosper *as we work diligently with the gifts and abilities God has given us.* God can give us supernatural favor, *even in the eyes of unbelievers,* **as we walk in love!**

God wants to prosper us, but don't be deceived into thinking we can be blessed while *never* putting our hand to what God has told us to do. Proverbs 10:4 says, *"He who has a slack hand becomes poor, but the hand of the diligent makes rich."*

Godly Character is the Key

A man asked God how long a million years was to Him.

God replied, "It's just like a single second of your time, my child."

So the man asked, "What about a million dollars?"

The Lord replied, "To me, it's just like a single penny."

The man gathered himself up and said, "Well, Lord, could I have one of your pennies?" and God said, "Certainly, my child, just a second." [14]

What if we *never* become rich? **Is becoming rich our reason for serving God?** Or, do we serve God because we love Him and we want to bring honor to His name? **I am not anti-prosperity.** I simply think that our **#1** priority in life *has to be* **our relationship with God**. I don't see anywhere in the Bible where *wealth* is of *primary* importance. Our primary focus as Christians *must be* our **relationship with God**!

God's Word shows us that He will give us great favor, guide and direct our paths, and bless us through supernatural means as we put into practice the biblical principles of tithing, giving offerings above and beyond the tithe, sowing and reaping, *and* **proper work ethics**. I do believe God wants to prosper us according to His Word. (See Malachi 3:8-11, Joshua 1:7, and Proverbs 10:4.)

---

[14] *Ibid.,* Michael Hodgin.

Prosperity, according to the Word of God, is an *outgrowth* of our relationship with the Father and our obedience to His Word. What do many people think of when they hear the word *prosperity*? For many Christians it conveys the idea of substantial wealth. However, when the Bible speaks of *prosperity* it's talking about having **all our needs met**. In 3 John 2, where John says "I pray that you may **prosper in all things**...," the word "prosper" is the Greek word *euodoo*. Euodoo literally means to help on the road or succeed in reaching.

Does having our needs met automatically mean being a millionaire? I do believe God will meet all of our needs as we serve Him, and that we will even have an overflow so we can be a blessing to others. God can make us very prosperous.

Maybe God *will* make the way for us to become wealthy. However, I also believe God would be doing *any of us* a great disservice if He didn't first develop in us the *character required to handle such wealth in a godly manner.* For example: What if I gave my six-year-old a $100 bill? I'll tell you what will happen — I'll find it on the floor in his bedroom. At this point in his life he's not mature enough to handle that kind of money. He doesn't have the maturity to properly discern its value, and therefore he's not capable of being a good steward.

Many times we do newborn babes in Christ (as Peter calls them) a great disservice by preaching the prosperity message without telling them they must focus on walking in godly character *first*. Of course, *God will* take care of His newborns just like good earthly parents take care of theirs. But, will He entrust them with great wealth? He won't if it means potential ruin of their spiritual walk.

Think about this: what would happen if suddenly every person in your church was given a million dollars? My guess is, you probably wouldn't see *at least* half of them the next Sunday. Our heavenly Father would never do anything to ruin us. God can only prosper us in accordance with what our maturity level *in Him* can handle.

Does it have to be a choice? Can we have both godly character *and* great prosperity? Absolutely! Here's what it boils down to: It's up to us whether or not we mature and grow strong in the character of God. It's our responsibility to keep our priorities in check. So, what does it take to obtain, *and maintain,* biblical prosperity? **Godly character!** "Be in health and prosper *even as your **soul** prospers."*

> *This Book of the Law shall not depart from your mouth, but you shall meditate in it day and night, that you may observe to do according to all that is written in it. For then you will make your way prosperous, and then you will have good success.*
>
> *Joshua 1:8*

How do we have good success and prosperity? **When we meditate in the Word day and night, and observe to do all that is written in it.**

Jesus talks about keeping up with the Joneses in Matthew 6:28-34: *"So why do you worry about clothing? Consider the lilies of the field, how they grow: they neither toil nor spin; and yet I say to you that even Solomon in all his glory was not arrayed like one of these. Now if God so clothes the grass of the field, which today is, and tomorrow is thrown into the oven, will he not much more clothe you, **O you of little faith?** Therefore do not worry, saying, 'What shall we eat?' or 'What shall we wear?' **For after all these things the Gentiles*** **[unbelievers]** ***seek.** For your heavenly*

Father knows that you need all these things. ***But seek first the kingdom of God and His righteousness, and all these things shall be added to you.*** *Therefore do not worry about tomorrow, for tomorrow will worry about its own things. Sufficient for the day is its own trouble."*

It sounds like Jesus had a problem with people who worry about and seek after *things*. He called them people of "little faith." God is not against wealth unless it impairs your relationship with Him. Jesus says *if we'll seek first His kingdom,* **and His righteousness,** then all those *things* will be added to us. That's the same principle He imparted to Joshua.

We need to ask ourselves, *"Who are the Joneses anyway?" Who are these people who can cause someone to abandon their relationship with God?* We need to forget about keeping up with the Joneses! We need to keep up with what God wants to do in our lives, seek His kingdom and His righteousness, and live a godly life! Then, who knows, *the Joneses may end up coming to church with us.*

WEALTH AT THE EXPENSE OF OUR RELATIONSHIP WITH GOD IS NOT WORTH WHAT IT WILL COST FOR ALL ETERNITY!

Chapter 10

Conclusion

Famous Last Words

You know you're getting older when:

Everything hurts, and what doesn't hurt, doesn't work.
The gleam in your eyes is from the sun hitting your bifocals.
You get winded playing chess.
Your children begin to look middle-aged.
You join a health club and don't go.
You decide to procrastinate but never get around to it.
Your mind makes contracts your body can't meet.
You look forward to a dull evening at home.
You're turning out the lights for economic reasons rather than romantic reasons.

Your knees buckle and your belt won't.
You sink your teeth in a steak and they stay there. [15]

Have you ever noticed how difficult it is to convince people who are in their early 20s and 30s that they need to give their lives to God? I've heard it said that if you don't reach people while they are young (grade school or high school age) that it becomes increasingly more difficult as they get older. John Mason said, "Too many people have *only an interest* in their destiny." I would extrapolate from that, that too many people have *only an interest* in God.

I'm amazed *(indeed, very bothered)* at how many times I've had discussions with people about God and I make statements or ask questions that, in my opinion, demand a response. Questions like: "Don't you believe that the Bible is the Word of God?" Or, "**You do** believe in heaven and hell, **don't you**?" Instead of a response they turn away, or stick their noses back in their newspaper or magazine.

It's sad to say, but many people would rather stick their heads in the sand and hope that there isn't a God. Or if there is a God they hope He won't send them to hell — because overall they've been a *pretty good person*.

Why do people act this way? I believe one of the biggest reasons is selfishness. As I've already mentioned, *to some folks,* believing in God and truly turning their lives over to Him would be a major inconvenience. All that "church stuff" takes up way too much time! And, it would spoil all of their fun — so they think. This person might say to himself, *"If there is a God I'll just give my*

---

[15] *Parables, Etc.*, July 1982.

life to Him when I'm old." That way he can have his cake and eat it too. The fallacy in that type of thinking is that he has no guarantee he will live that long. Even if a person does, who says his logic will change when he becomes old?

I will share a story with you to help illustrate my point. This is a story about a man named Cyrus Wellington. (**Note:** Even though this is a fictional story, Cyrus Wellington's name has been changed to protect his anonymity.) See if this story sounds familiar. Maybe you know someone who's lived this life, or something similar.

When Cyrus was in his early 20s, with a whole life of possibilities in front of him, he saw little need for accepting Jesus as his Savior. It was an extremely selfish time in his life. He graduated from college and began his career. He worked hard and began making a lot of money. It felt good to be on his own! He thrust himself into acquiring material possessions. He also began to look for Ms. Right. This led to several failed relationships. He saw women only as objects, or a prize to be obtained. He felt no remorse for his manipulation.

However, soon he found the *perfect* relationship, and coupled with his ongoing accumulation of material possessions, this led to total happiness — or so he believed. Despite an occasional bad circumstance or two, at that point in his life he felt indestructible. Cyrus was on top of the world! There was no need for God. And then, the bottom fell out!

Now in his late 20s the honeymoon was over. He spent too much time on his career, and not enough time caring for his family. He became very disillusioned. He couldn't understand why his wife — *all of a sudden* — had different dreams and goals. He thought she understood what was most important to him. Wrapped up in his selfishness his anger grew. A couple of years later he filed for divorce. Surprisingly, Cyrus still saw no need for God. He was young, he was strong, and he was convinced he could pull himself up by his own bootstraps.

Once again he was footloose, and fancy free. However, now he had acquired an ex-wife as well as an alimony and child support payment that took one third of his paycheck each month. But he wasn't discouraged! He was only thirty-two and he had his whole life ahead of him.

Back in the dating scene he swore he would never make the same mistake twice. He continued to work hard and climb the company ladder. He was quite the playboy. He had a nice condo, a nice car, and a beautiful girlfriend he used and manipulated. He also had a daughter he saw four times a month so he could salve his conscience and reassure himself that he was a good father. Still, Cyrus saw no need for God.

As he approached forty, the unexpected happened! He fell in love. He struggled with the idea of entering into another marriage. He said to himself, *"But I've changed. I'm a different man. I can do it right this time. After all, this woman is much more mature than my ex-wife. She sees things my way."*

So he married his dream lover who was ten years younger than he was, and had a child from a previous marriage. She made him feel young and virile, and his new stepson adored him. Now with the perfect wife and family, and a management position in the company, he was on top of the world. There was certainly no need for God at this point in his life!

Things rolled along fairly well for about ten years. Cyrus worked harder than ever so that he could retire in ten or fifteen years with a substantial amount of wealth. His stepson was now a teenager and had not received the fatherly guidance he needed. As a result of the neglect, his stepson became increasingly rebellious. His stepson's rebellious antics played havoc with Cyrus' time and finances, and took him away from the ongoing pursuit of wealth and material possessions. His stepson resented the material possessions that had pilfered his stepfather's love and attention. The stepson increased in his destructive behavior. Cyrus' selfish heart once again led him to begin divorce proceedings.

After his second divorce, Cyrus finally began to feel a need for spiritual enlightenment to comfort his wounded soul. His selfish motive notwithstanding, it was a step in the right direction. In his spare time, he looked into various religions, but was careful to conceal his investigation from friends and co-workers for fear of ridicule.

His private search for inner peace was made public after one of his co-workers saw a Bible on his desk. Cyrus discovered very quickly that *everyone* had an opinion. After many ardent barroom discussions, and various books about psychics and new age philosophies (donated by "concerned" co-workers), his search for spirituality became clouded. It wasn't long before Cyrus abandoned his search, and his hopes quickly diminished.

Due to his divorce settlements, his finances were not what he had hoped they would be as he approached sixty. His employer pressured him to retire. He stayed on as long as he could, but the pressure grew stronger as the company searched for a younger executive to step into his position. Cyrus held on to his position for five more years, then he allowed the company to buy him out.

Now, at age sixty-five, he also discovered that female companionship was difficult to find. Retired and lonely, he relished the short, sporadic visits from his daughter with whom he only enjoyed a cordial relationship. Approaching seventy, Cyrus looked back at his life and dreamed of what it could have been had he done things differently. He asked himself, *"Where did I go wrong?"* He also pondered questions like: *Is there another life after this? Is there really a God?*

For all of you who love happy endings, and because I am an eternal optimist, I'll end this story on a happy note:

Fortunately, Cyrus got invited to a vibrant, on fire church where the people loved God and extended His love to all they came in contact with. The first service he attended, Cyrus rushed to the front during the altar call weeping and repenting. He gave his heart to the Lord, and once again his world was new and exciting. The last 18 years of his life were the best he'd ever experienced. He forgave his ex-wives, renewed his relationship with his stepson and daughter, and they all got born again.

I know what you're saying. "That was a long, boring, and generic story." That, of course, is the point. Brevity may be the soul of wit, but sometimes a long boring story helps drive home a point. It can be an illustration of a long wearisome life of searching for happiness through the selfish pursuit of material possessions and fleshly satisfaction. And unfortunately, many of the real life Cyrus Wellingtons don't turn their lives over to God before they die. Too often it's just the opposite. Their hearts become hard and they die in their sin.

When we're young we feel as though we're indestructible. As we get older we take control of our lives and are guided according to our gifts and abilities. We strive for success, sometimes even at the expense of family and friends.

Consider what James 4:13-17 says: *"Come now, you who say, 'Today or tomorrow we will go to such and such a city, spend a year there, buy and sell and make a profit'; whereas you do not know what will happen tomorrow. For what is your life?* ***It is even a vapor that appears for a little time and then vanishes away.*** *Instead you ought to say, 'If the Lord wills, we shall live and do this or that.' But now you boast in your arrogance. All such boasting is evil. Therefore, to him who knows to do good and does not do it, to him it is sin."*

God will not ask us to do anything He has not created us to do. If we will seek God's will for our lives, we will not only find life enjoyable, but we will realize the true purpose for which God created us. A Christian who follows God's plans and purposes **will not** look back at life and see a dull meaningless facade full of heartache and misery.

In spite of the inevitable trials and tribulations, the Christian life is anything but dull. Even in the midst of hard times a person who puts his trust in God can have peace in his heart, and confidence that God hears and answers. Without God, even if we live a relatively joyous life as a *good person*, we will always have that nagging feeling that there's something more. There will always be those questions in our mind; *"Is there a God?" — "Is the Bible true?" — "Is there life after death?"*

Anatole France said, "The average man does not know what to do with this life, yet wants another one which will last forever." Accept the reality of heaven, hell, and a merciful forgiving God who sent His Son Jesus to this earth to die for our sins. He is the One who now sits at the right hand of the Father.

What proof do I have? A universe created with divine order. A solar system designed by an all-powerful Creator, and not accidentally manufactured out of chaos. The splendor and beauty of an earth which produces all the sustenance we need to sustain life. Male and female human beings who reproduce after their *own kind* **just as the Bible says**. The rich and miraculous history of the Judeo/ Christian faith backed up by thousands of historical documents and archaeological discoveries. And most of all, millions of lives that have been forever changed by the power of the Word of God, and the inward work of the Holy Spirit!

Everyone has to decide for themselves. We can't let our last words be "I wonder if there really is a God." We can know for sure. And we can begin to develop a close relationship with the One who created the heavens and the earth. Imagine that! The Almighty God, the Creator of everything, desires to have a personal relationship *with us*.

Sound to good to be true? Imagine having a close personal friend (closer than a brother) who's the most intelligent, most creative, most magnificent, most powerful being that has ever existed. And his father wants to adopt us into the family and make us a joint heir with his only son.

That is precisely the opportunity God has extended toward all who will believe. "Believe what?" you ask. Romans 10:9-10 says, *"That if you confess with your mouth the Lord Jesus and believe in your heart that God has raised Him from the dead, you will be saved. For with the heart one believes unto righteousness, and with the mouth confession is made unto salvation."*

If you're reading this and you've already made that decision then, *drive on my friend*! Live your life in the fullness and power of the Holy Spirit! But, if you're reading this and haven't made that decision, you can do it now. Simply pray this prayer *from your heart* — In other words don't just read these words, but pray them because *you have an assurance in your heart* that you believe!

Lord God, I believe Your Word which tells me that if I have confessed with my mouth that Jesus is Lord, and believe in my heart that You raised Him from the dead that I will be saved. Almighty God, I confess right now that I believe You sent Your Son Jesus into this world to die for my sins, I confess that Jesus is Lord, and I believe with all my heart that You raised Him from the dead. Now, according to Your Word, **I AM SAVED!**

If you just became a Christian — Congratulations! Go tell someone about it! Find a good church and get involved. Most importantly — NEVER TURN BACK! I pray that you will live your life in such a way that one day you will hear those coveted words from our Redeemer — ***"Well done, good and faithful servant"*** *(Matthew 25:21).*

Fill Me Up Lord

A crystal chalice waiting to be filled,
Beautiful crystal with ornate inlaid gold,
Created with brilliance by a loving Creator.
What substance will it contain?
New wine, or a poison bringing slow death.
Will the brilliant gold become tarnished and dull,
Or will it be polished with tender care?
When this life is over what will it's legacy be?
O Beautiful crystal what will they say of thee?
Will they say, "You were a gift in the hand of the Father,
And served many by refreshing their soul?"
Or, will they say, "What was born in beauty was neglected and broken, and what remained grew old and was lost forever."
O Father fill me up!
Fill me till I overflow!
Make me a blessing, a gift to all who are thirsty.
So that those whose lives I touch will see,
The glorious reflection of my Creator in me!

Appendix A

(aahh…my appendix!)

The Word Under Glass

(part 1)

Taste and see that the Lord is good.
— Psalm 34:8

These appendices may not contain as many humorous anecdotes as the guts of the book, but bear with me! I couldn't resist the title! In contrast though, this part of the book will probably resemble a barbecue more than a gourmet dinner.

Nevertheless, I hope that it will not only be palatable, but also that it will give you some insight into the incredible depth of the eternal best seller. The book that has been printed in more languages and is unmatched in worldwide distribution. You know the one, don't you? The gigantic black book your aunt Mildred has on her coffee table (on top of a lace doily, next to some plastic flowers) with the big gold letters on the front that shout, "HOLY BIBLE."

My heart's desire is that you'll discover what a fascinating book the Bible is, and realize that you can understand it. Though most of all, I pray that you will recognize God's hand as He composed this amazing book just for you!

The Old Testament

The Old Testament begins with the **book of Genesis**. In the Greek, *Genesis* means: origin or beginning (imagine that). Tradition accredits Moses as the author of Genesis and the next four books; Exodus, Leviticus, Numbers, and Deuteronomy. Together, the first five books of the Bible are called the Pentateuch (Pentatook), meaning "Five Scrolls." These are the major events which occur in the book of Genesis:

- The creation of heaven, earth, and life upon the earth.
- The fall of man (Adam and Eve get groceries from the wrong tree).
- Noah and the Flood.
- The Abrahamic Covenant (God's lifelong friendship and vow of inheritance to Abraham and his descendants).
- The life of Abraham's son Isaac; Isaac's sons, Esau and Jacob; and Jacob's twelve sons who sire the twelve tribes of Israel.

The book of Genesis ends with the story of Jacob's son, Joseph, being sold into slavery, Joseph's rise to power in Egypt, and the reconciliation of his family as he is able to save them from a great famine in Egypt. Genesis is a fascinating book full of pre-flood history, and foreshadowings of the coming Messiah (Jesus) even thousands of years before Christ was born into this earth via the virgin Mary.

And, if you've ever wondered how science and dinosaurs harmonize with the biblical account of creation, I recommend the following websites: **www.drdino.com**., and **www.icr.org**.

In the book of Genesis, God makes a promise to Abraham to bless his descendants and give to them a special land for an inheritance. This of course became known as — that's right, the Promised Land.

At the beginning of the next book, **Exodus,** we see that a new generation (of Egyptians) had risen to power in Egypt *"and they did not remember Joseph."* As a result, God's people became slaves to the Egyptians. These are the major events that occur in the book of Exodus.

- Oppression of the Israelite slaves in Egypt.
- Birth and early life of Moses.
- The plagues on the Egyptians and the deliverance process.
- The Exodus event.
- Miraculous crossing of the Red Sea.
- The Ten Commandments given.
- The golden calf incident.
- God miraculously guides Israel, and miraculously feeds Israel.
- The construction of the Tabernacle in the Wilderness.

The next book is the **book of Leviticus**. The English title "Leviticus" is derived from the Greek version of the work, and means matters pertaining to the Levites. And right now you're saying, "WHAT IN THE WORLD ARE LEVITES?" Levites were the priests who performed the sacrifices and the various priestly duties in the newly built wilderness tabernacle (which was basically a portable temple, or M*A*S*H — **M**obile **A**rmy **S**ynagogue for the **H**ebrews).

Leviticus is simply Moses spelling out all the sundry sacrificial duties and services of the priests pertaining to the different types of sacrificial offerings from the people of Israel (that was easy for me to say!). Moses also covers holy days, laws for elements of worship, laws of impurities, blessings for obedience, and punishment for disobedience.

If you've never read the book of Leviticus, I would highly recommend it. Be prepared because it is different, and if you're a new Christian I would not start with the book of Leviticus (start in the book of John). Before you read Leviticus (or the Bible for that matter), I would strongly suggest a Bible such as: the New King James Version (no thees or thous). It's also to your advantage to have a Bible with a good commentary and study notes.

In the book of Leviticus, you can quickly see that no one on the face of the earth could keep this very strict and complicated law. That was God's whole point! Since the beginning, God has desired to have a *relationship* with his wonderful human creation.

It's very sad that man has habitually desired to know exactly where the line is that he cannot cross. Not so that he can stay as far away from that line as possible, but so he can push sin to its extreme limits. So God, through Moses, creates a law that no human being could possibly live by, to drive home the point that man *could not* do it on his own. Man needed a Savior. In this system God set up, we can see the stage being set for the final sacrifice — the cross of redemption.

We see again that even thousands of years before Christ came, God was revealing clues, hints, and foreshadowings of the miraculous work He would do through His Son Jesus! Once again you can see how only an all-knowing, all-powerful God put together such a book! It's been said that "In the Old the New is contained, and in the New the Old is explained."

In the **book of Numbers** the children of Israel are still in the "Wilderness of Sinai." Here are the major events in the book of Numbers.

- Census of military and nonmilitary people.
- Dedicating of the Levites, and the Second Passover.
- Guidance by cloud and fire.
- Rebellion and punishment of the first generation.
- Moses and Aaron's leadership is challenged.
- Balaam's donkey that God makes talk.
- Preparation and census of the new generation.

By now the Israelites had turned a relatively short journey, from the Red Sea to Canaan (the Promised Land), into many years of whining and complaining in the wilderness of Sinai. Because of their doubt and unbelief (doubting that God would do as He had promised), God tells them that the whole generation He delivered out of Egypt will pass away in the wilderness.

The next book, **Deuteronomy**, is a series of farewell addresses by Moses to the Israelites. As Moses prepares to die, the new generation prepares to enter the Promised Land. Moses tells them thirty-five times to "go in and possess the land." Moses' messages consist of:

- The past remembered.
- A call of obedience.
- Exposition of the Ten Commandments, ceremonial laws, civil laws, criminal laws, and social laws.
- Restating of God's covenant with Israel.
- Perpetuation of that covenant.
- Moses' blessing on Israel
- Moses inaugurates his successor, Joshua and Moses' death.

The **book of Joshua** (authorship uncertain) opens at the doorstep of Israel's entrance into Canaan. The book of Joshua is the first in a group of books called the Former Prophets. Collectively, these books tell of the development of God's kingdom in the Promised Land until they enter into Babylonian captivity (a period of 900 years). These are some of the major events in the book of Joshua:

- The miraculous crossing of the Jordan.
- Joshua meets the Commander of the Lord's Army (the preincarnate Christ) face to face.
- The two spies spy out Jericho and make a vow of safety to Rahab the harlot and her family.
- Jericho's walls fall, Jericho is utterly destroyed by Israel.
- Defeat at Ai, and Achan's sin.
- Victory at Ai, and Joshua is deceived by the Gibeonites.
- Joshua commands the sun and moon to stand still until the Amorites are defeated.
- The land is divided.

- Joshua gives his final discourse, counsels the leaders, challenges the people, then dies.

The **book of Judges** (author unknown) covers the period between Joshua's death and the rise of the monarchy. The book of Judges covers a chaotic period in Israel's history from about 1380 to 1050 BC. Under the leadership of Joshua, Israel had generally conquered and occupied the land of Canaan, but large areas remained yet to be possessed by the individual tribes of Israel.

By deliberately serving foreign gods, the people of Israel broke their covenant with the Lord. As a result, each time the people cried out to the Lord, He faithfully raised up a judge to bring deliverance to His people. These judges whom God raised up and anointed with His Spirit were military and civil leaders. Here are some of the things you will find in the book of Judges:

- The conditions of Canaan after the death of Joshua.
- Continuing conquest by the Israelite tribes.
- The covenant of the Lord broken.
- Deliverance from oppression by Ehud, Shamgar, Deborah, Barak, Gideon, and Jephthah.
- Judgeships of Tola, Jair, Ibzan, and Elon.
- Philistine oppression and the exploits of Samson.
- The idolatry of Micah and the migration of the Danites.
- The atrocity at Gibeah and the Benjamite war.

I know you're thinking that all those weird names and situations sound so appealing to read about. The book of Judges, however, gives you a true sense of the mercy and forgiveness of God. Over and over again, God's people committed idolatry by whoring after others gods. Because of their sin they were oppressed by other nations. The fact that God did not give up on them reveals the hope we can have for the lost and backslidden even today.

Following Judges is the **book of Ruth**. The book of Ruth is a story which displays the sovereignty of God. The book of Ruth speaks of the long-suffering and mercy of God, which brings an end to a story that begins with famine, death, and loss. The book also shows that God's protective covering, and His divine promises are for those who remain *obedient to Him*. When you read the book of Ruth remember that in His almighty state of being, God is not *opposed* to man, but He continually proves Himself to be man's *deliverer*.

Johann Wolfgang von Goethe, the German writer-poet, described Ruth as "the loveliest complete work on a small scale." Some have called the book of Ruth the "Crown Jewel of the Old Testament." It's not only a literary masterpiece, but a record of the genealogy of David, the crowned king of Israel who is also in the bloodline of Jesus.

First and Second Samuel were originally one book called "The Book of Samuel." In **1 Samuel** you see how Israel, which had been governed by judges who God had raised up at crucial times in the nation's history, had deteriorated both morally and politically. Samuel, the prophet of God, steps into this corrupt and confusing time.

When Samuel grows old the nation beseeches him to give them a king. God did not want them to have a king, but Israel wanted to be like all the other nations. (See 1 Samuel 8:20.) God took this as a personal rejection. (See 1 Samuel 8:7.) There is such danger in conformity, and God was saying, **"I don't want you to be like the world, I want you to serve Me!"** First Samuel contains:

- Birth and childhood of Samuel.
- Beginning of Samuel's ministry, capture and recovery of the ark, Samuel's call for repentance, defeat of the Philistines.
- Saul's establishment as king of Israel, Saul's wars, and Saul's rejection by God.
- David's rise to prominence, David's anointing by Samuel, David's defeat of Goliath.
- Saul's persecution of David, Saul's visit to a fortuneteller, David's conflicts with the Amalekites, and Saul's death.

Second Samuel deals with David's rise to the throne of Israel and the forty years of his reign. David is the focal point of 2 Samuel. Highlights of the book of 2 Samuel:

- The troubles in David's house (Nathan's prophecy, death of David's son, incest in David's house).
- The troubles in David's kingdom.

First and Second Kings were originally one book which formed a sequel to 1 and 2 Samuel. The books of 1 and 2 Kings take up the recording of the historical events of God's people where the books of 1 and 2 Samuel leave off. However, 1 and 2 Kings is a selective history with a theological purpose, and not a chronological history. The author (attributed to Jeremiah) brings out people and events that are morally and religiously significant. 1 and 2 Kings present *God* as the *Lord of history*. Significant events in 1 and 2 Kings are:

- The establishment of Solomon as King.
- The building of Solomon's temple.

- The kingdom is divided. (Can you guess over what issue the kingdom of Israel split? For the answer see the end of the chapter.)
- The reigns of the various kings of the divided kingdom.

Like Samuel, and Kings, **1 and 2 Chronicles** were originally one book called "Events of the Days." Its authorship is attributed to Ezra. The word "chronicle" means a record of events, or history. The book of 1 Chronicles covers a period from Adam to the death of David around 971 BC. Minus the genealogies in 1 Chronicles 1-9, 1 and 2 Chronicles cover roughly the same period of time as 1 and 2 Kings. It's a duplication of, and a supplement to 1 and 2 Samuel and 1 and 2 Kings. First and Second Chronicles covers:

- The roots of God's people.
- The reign of King David.
- The reign of King Solomon.
- The reigns of the kings of Judah.
- Judah's captivity and return.

The **book of Ezra** (probably written by Ezra — *brilliant deduction, Jeff!*) covers slightly more than eighty years. The name Ezra likely means "The Lord Has Helped." The Hebrew bible recognized Ezra-Nehemiah as a single book. Ezra himself was a *"priest, a scribe, expert in the words of the commandments of the Lord*" (Ezra 7:11). Here are some major events in Ezra:

- The end of captivity in Babylon.
- Israel's return under Zerubbabel.
- The temple reconstruction process.
- The exiles return under Ezra.
- Ezra's reform as Ezra confesses Israel's transgressions.

Nehemiah is a tremendous book, exemplifying great leadership and cooperation during a very stressful undertaking. The book is named after its main character who displays many outstanding qualities of leadership such as organizational skills, and confidence in God's plans and purposes. Nehemiah also exhibits amazing spiritual depth as he fasts, prays, and is immediately responsive to God's direction.

Nehemiah shows the practical everyday side of our faith as he takes on the challenge of rebuilding Jerusalem's wall. During this project, we see how a man of God operates in helping his workers overcome laziness while enduring through mocking, physical threats, and even conspiracy. The major events in Nehemiah are:

- Nehemiah goes from exile to rebuild the walls of Jerusalem.
- Ezra and Nehemiah work together to establish the people.
- True repentance results in righteousness.

The **book of Esther** is a graphic account relating how God's people were saved from ruin during the fifth century BC. The name of the book comes from a beautiful, orphaned Jewess who became the queen of the Persian king Ahasuerus. Esther is a study in the survival of God's people in the midst of hostility. A peculiar feature of Esther is that the name of God is not mentioned. But God's unmistakable hand print can been seen throughout the book of Esther. Main features of the book of Esther are:

- A new queen is chosen.
- The king's life is saved.
- A plot against the Jews is formed.

- Mordecai is exalted.
- Haman is hanged.

The authorship of the **book of Job** is uncertain. Scripture itself attest that Job was a real person. He is referred to in Ezekiel 14:14 and James 5:11. Job was a wealthy man living somewhat of a nomadic life. The book of Job has been called "a dramatic poem framed in an epic story." The meaning of the book of Job is one of the most debated topics in Christianity. Major events in Job are:

- Satan challenges Job's character and destroys everything Job has.
- Dialogue between Job and his friends.
- Job addresses his friends.
- Elihu challenges Job.
- God's address from the whirlwind.
- Job's response.

The **book of Psalms** is a compilation of several ancient collections of Hebrew songs and poetry. The main authors are David, Asaph, and the Sons of Korah. The book of Psalms is full of wonderful praise and thanksgiving *to* God. Psalms also elucidates many of God's promises to man.

Proverbs was written by Solomon, with portions by Agur and King Lemuel. God told Solomon, *"There has not been anyone like you before you, nor shall any like you arise after you" (1 Kings 3:12).* Proverbs is full of **great wisdom**. You'll also notice that there are thirty-one chapters in the book of Proverbs. That means you can read one chapter each day of the month.

> *The words of the Preacher, the son of David, king in Jerusalem. "Vanity of vanities," says the Preacher; "Vanity of vanities, all is vanity."*
>
> *Ecclesiastes 1:1-2*

Those are the first words of the **book of Ecclesiastes**. The name *Ecclesiastes* is derived from the Greek word, *ekklesia* ("assembly"), and means one who addresses an assembly. The Hebrew word so represented is *qoheleth*, which means one who convenes an assembly, thus often being rendered "Teacher" or "Preacher" in English versions.

The writing of **Ecclesiates** is generally credited to Solomon (about 971 to 931 BC), and is believed to have been written in his old age. Many believe the pessimistic tone of the book is in keeping with Solomon's spiritual state at the time he wrote it.

The "Preacher" is determined to find the real value of life. Solomon explores all the avenues of pleasure, work, accomplishments, wealth, life, death, and everything "done under the sun." Solomon discovers that in the grand scheme of things it is all *vanity*, and *"grasping at the wind."* In Ecclesiates 12:13 Solomon says, *"Let us hear the conclusion of the whole matter: Fear God and keep His commandments, for this is man's all."*

Some may see Ecclesiates as having little value because it was written during Solomon's *apparent* apostate condition. I look at it somewhat differently. I believe the book of Ecclesiastes can be a great help, particularly in witnessing to an unsaved person or a backslidden Christian. *Because, Solomon did all the research for us!*

The **Song of Solomon** is attributed to…Yep, Solomon. *Love* is the key word in the song. The Song of Solomon depicts a beautiful parallel between the covenant of love between man and wife, and the love relationship enjoyed by God's church.

The first verse of **the book of Isaiah** names its author — Isaiah. The name "Isaiah" means "Yahweh Is Salvation." Isaiah is directly quoted twenty-one times in the New Testament. Isaiah was a prophet during the reigns of Uzziah, Jotham, Ahaz, and Hezekiah who were kings of Judah. (See Isaiah 1:1.)

One of Isaiah's purposes was to declare how displeased God was, and to declare God's judgment on sin in Judah, Israel, and the surrounding nations. Isaiah's greatest purpose, however, was to establish a groundwork of hope and promise for the faithful remnant of God's people. Isaiah prophesied both the first advent of Christ as well as the second advent of Christ.

Jeremiah is sometimes called "the Weeping Prophet." He displayed great compassion for his people and wept over them. Jeremiah was a prophet during the reign of Josiah; his three sons — Jehoahaz, Jehoiakim, and Zedekiah; and a grandson — Jehoiachin. Even though Jeremiah was compassionate, he condemned the idolatry among the people and proclaimed severe judgment unless the people repented. The message of Jeremiah is more than relevant, *especially today*. Sin must be punished, true repentance brings restoration, and obedience leads to blessing and joy.

Tradition says that Jeremiah also wrote the **book of Lamentations**. There are six major themes in the book of Lamentations all joined with the idea of suffering: Israel's suffering was the result of their sin.

- The Babylonians were nothing more than an instrument in the hand of God.
- Their suffering could direct them *toward* God.
- Suffering, tears, and prayer belong together.
- Prayer should always be rooted in *faith and hope*.
- Their responsibility was to acquiesce to their sufferings patiently.

Ezekiel, which means "God Strengthens," was the son of Buzi (nice name!) and his prophetic ministry briefly overlapped Jeremiah's. His prophetic message was to the immoral remnant of Judah which was exiled in Babylon. Ezekiel's main message is the moral responsibility of each individual. We cannot ride to heaven on someone else's coattails, or likewise, blame our failures on the shortcomings of others. Here are some of the events in the book of Ezekiel:

- The vision and call of Ezekiel.
- Oracles of judgment against Jerusalem, then the whole nation.
- Judah's exile and captivity.
- Message of judgment against Judah.
- Oracles of doom against foreign nations.
- Prophecies of restoration.

Daniel was deported as a teenager in 605 BC to Babylon where he lived over sixty years. At first Daniel served as a trainee in Nebuchanezzar's court. Later, he became an advisor to foreign kings. The book of Daniel was written by Daniel and it has three main sections.

1. Introduction to the person of Daniel.
2. Daniel's key test of character and the development of his prophetic interpretation skills.
3. Daniel's series of visions about future kingdoms and events.

The book of Daniel also contains many keys to help unlock the mysteries of subjects such as the Antichrist, the Great Tribulation, and the second coming of Christ. Here are some key events in the book of Daniel:

- Nebuchanezzar's first dream.
- Deliverance from the fiery furnace.
- Nebuchanezzar's second dream.
- Belshazzar's blasphemous feast.
- Daniel in the lions' den.
- Daniel's first vision and second vision.
- Prophecy of the seventy weeks.
- Daniel's final vision.

The **book of Hosea**, written by…Hosea, is about a people who needed to hear the love of God. God showed his love for them in a very unique way. God allowed Hosea to be *a living illustration* of what God was saying to His people. In short, Hosea marries an impure woman, demonstrates great love toward her and has children by her, then goes after her to bring her back when she goes astray. Hosea shows by his love for his wife, the type of love God had for Israel. Major events in the book of Hosea:

- Hosea's marriage to Gomer.
- Hosea's taking back of Gomer.
- Sin of Israel and judgment of Israel.
- Love and restoration.

Joel literally means "Yahweh is God". The **book of Joel** probably takes place around 835-805 BC during a time of great devastation to the entire land of Judah. Joel is divided into two sections. The first section deals with the present judgment of God, a call to repentance, and a promise of restoration. The second section, the plague, horrible as it might have been, was nothing compared to the judgment of God that is coming. The major events in Joel are:

- The destruction by the locust.
- The repentance of Judah.
- The restoration of the Lord.
- The Lord's day in the future.

The **book of Amos** (written by Amos) takes place during the reigns of Uzziah of Judah and Jeroboam II of Israel (760-750 BC). Amos means "Burden-Bearer." Amos was called to proclaim God's message to the northern kingdom of Israel. The book of Amos is basically a message of judgment, though in the end Amos promises restoration of Israel. Major events in Amos are:

- Judgment on the nations.
- Oracles against Israel.
- Visions of Judgment
- Restoration of Israel.

The theme of the **book of Obadiah** is God's judgment on Edom, and it's the shortest book in the Old Testament. The book was written by Obadiah, whose name means "Servant/Worshiper of Yahweh." More than ten men are named Obadiah in the Old Testament. One tradition connects the author of this prophecy with the Obadiah identified as King Ahab's steward. Other than speculation, nothing else is known about Obadiah. Obadiah's prophecy is directed toward the people mourning over the ruin of the city of Jerusalem and the deaths of family, friends, and relatives. The book of Obadiah contains:

- Edom's condemnation, collapse, and crimes.
- The day of divine retribution, restitution, and divine rule.

The theme of the **book of Jonah** is God's compassion for all men. Jonah prophesied during the reign of Jeroboam II and immediately preceding Amos. He was the only prophet sent to preach to the Gentiles. Jonah had a difficult time accepting the fact that God would show mercy to Nineveh of Assyria when he thought they deserved severe judgment. The book of Jonah is different from other prophetic books because instead of prophecies that contain a message, the story itself is the message. Events in Jonah are:

- God calls Jonah to go to Nineveh.
- Jonah flees to Tarshish.
- The Lord sends a storm, Jonah's thrown overboard, the Lord sends a great fish.
- Jonah repents and goes to Nineveh to preach.
- Jonah is angry and God teaches Jonah a lesson.

Micah was a contemporary with Isaiah and Hosea in the 8th century before Christ. Micah's name means "He Who is Like Yahweh." The **book of Micah** is a prophecy about the Lord who can be compared with *no one* when it comes to forgiving sins and having compassion on sinners.

The message of Micah is centered around one theme: "Who is a God like You, pardoning iniquity and passing over the transgression of the remnant of His heritage?" Major events in Micah are:

- The Lord's dramatic coming in judgment.
- The Lord's condemnation of the leadership.
- The Lord's coming universal kingdom.
- The Lord's presentation of His case.
- The Lord's salvation as the nation's hope.

The **book of Nahum** focuses on a single concern: the fall of the city of Nineveh. Nahum means "Comforter" or "Full of Comfort." Nahum is the author and it was most likely written shortly before 612 BC There are three major sections to Nahum's prophecy.

1. The first describes God's great power and how it works to give protection to the righteous and judgment for wickedness.
2. The second section describes the coming destruction of Nineveh.
3. The third section shows how, even though God's judgment is severe, He is justified in His condemnation of wickedness.

Habakkuk lived during one of Judah's most crucial periods. The world around Judah was at war. The **book of Habakkuk** was probably written between the fall of Nineveh (612 BC) and the fall of Jerusalem (586 BC). Habakkuk tells of a spiritual trek from doubt to worship. Habakkuk shows us that it's not necessarily a lack of faith to ask God, *"Why?"* Habakkuk doesn't deny his circumstances, but rather finds God to be everything he needs in times of trouble. Habakkuk contains:

- Habakkuk's questions.
- God's answer.
- Habakkuk's prayer.

As with most of the prophets, the **book of Zephaniah** contains three sections:

1. The pronouncement of judgment for sin;
2. A call for repentance;
3. God's promises of salvation to those who trusted in God.

Zephaniah, which means "The Lord Has Hidden," vividly describes the wrath of God, *and* the joy of God. Zephaniah himself states that he prophesied "in the days of Josiah, the son of Amon, King of Judah." Major events in Zephaniah are:

- The day of judgment against Judah.
- The day of the Lord.
- A call to repentance.
- Judgment against surrounding nations and Jerusalem.
- God Himself celebrates.

The theme of the **book of Haggai** is the rebuilding of the temple. Haggai, whose name means "Festive," prophesied around the same time as Zechariah. Haggai's ministry covers a period of less than four months during the second year of the reign of King Darius (520 BC). Haggai speaks of three issues common to all mankind:

1. Disinterest.
2. Discouragement.

3. Dissatisfaction.

Haggai also shows that we need each other in order to fulfill God's collective will for His people. Haggai's three sections:

- The Lord's first message: Consider your ways.
- The Lord's second message: Be strong and work.
- The Lord's third message: I will bless you.

Zechariah's prophetic ministry began in 520 BC, only two months after Haggai completed his prophecy. The **book of Zechariah** begins with a passionate word from the Lord for the people to repent and turn back to God. Zechariah means, "Yahweh Remembers," and he challenges the people of his time to complete the work that God has given them. God also reassures His people of His love and care through a series of eight visions. The contents of Zechariah are:

- The call to repentance.
- The eight visions.
- The crowning of the high priest.
- The restoration of Zion.
- The triumph of the kingdom of God.

The last book in the Old Testament is the **book of Malachi**. Malachi, whose name means "My Messenger," is not mentioned anywhere else in the Bible. Scholars believe he lived at the time of Nehemiah (450 BC). Malachi begins his book by laying a foundation of God's unwavering love for His people. Then Malachi rebukes God's people on several different fronts. He rebukes them for false religious practices, their denial of God's justice, and for robbing God of tithes and offerings. Malachi concludes with an exhortation to the people to "Remember the Law of Moses."

Question: Over what issue was the Kingdom of Israel divided?

Answer: ***Taxes*** *— Some things never change! (See 1 Kings chapter 12.)*

Appendix B

(my appendix feels better!)

The Word Under Glass

(part 2)

I hope this brief overview of the Bible has helped you understand the meaning of the books, how they relate to each other, *and* how each book helps complete the whole of the Word of God.

Between the Old and New Testament there was approximately four hundred years called the "silent period." At the close of the Old Testament, Persia had already been a world power for about one hundred years. They remained in power for another one hundred years until Alexander the Great, 336 BC, at the age of twenty, took the command of the Greek army and began to conquer the known world. Then came the Maccabean period of Independence, 167-63 BC. After that came the Roman period from 63 BC until the time of Christ.

Now let's take a look at an overview of the New Testament, and then some basic rules of Bible interpretation.

The New Testament

Matthew, Mark, Luke, and **John** are called the "Gospels," meaning "good news." These books are four different accounts of Jesus' life and ministry. It's similar to an attorney calling four different witnesses to testify in court. Each witnesses' testimony, *even though truthful*, may vary somewhat because the event is being viewed through four different pairs of eyes. Matthew, Mark, Luke, and John are all truthful testimonies of Jesus' life seen from different angles.

Early tradition unanimously names Matthew (the apostle and former tax collector) as the author of the gospel of Matthew. The gospel of Mark is believed to have been written by John Mark, a close associate of Peter and companion of Paul and Barnabas on their first missionary journey. The gospel of Luke is believed to have been written by Luke the physician, a close associate of Paul. Early church tradition says that John, "the beloved disciple," wrote the fourth gospel. This is the same John who "leaned upon His breast" at the last supper.

Matthew, Mark, and Luke are called the "synoptic" (similar) gospels. John, on the other hand, chose not to follow the same sequence of events you see in the first three gospels. The theme of the gospel of John is *Knowing God by Believing in Jesus Christ.* Considering that it's believed to have been written by the disciple who may have been closest to Jesus, it gives us an interesting perspective of the life of Christ. It's recommended many times that new believers start their Bible reading with the gospel of John.

Here's some of what you will find in the Gospels:

- Genealogy and infancy of Christ.
- The way is paved by John the Baptist.
- Jesus' public ministry, miracles, and teachings.
- Jesus' ministry to the disciples.
- The betrayal of Jesus.
- Jesus' death, burial, and resurrection.
- The Great Commission.

The **book of The Acts of the Apostles** begins with Jesus promising to send the Holy Spirit which will empower the New Testament church. Then we see Jesus ascending into heaven and an angel telling the disciples that the way He ascended, He will also return in a like manner. The book of Acts is a sequel to the life of Christ in the Gospels, and it records the spread of Christianity from Jerusalem to Rome.

Here are some significant events in the book of Acts:

- Jesus' promise to send the Holy Spirit.
- The outpouring of the Holy Spirit on the day of Pentecost.
- Peter's explanation and sermon to the confused crowd of which 3,000 get saved.
- The persecution and explosion of the new church after Pentecost.
- The ministry of Stephen and the conversion of Saul.

- The Council at Jerusalem to discuss law and grace.
- Paul's missionary journeys.

The **book of Romans** was written by the apostle Paul. Paul wrote to introduce himself to a church he had never visited, and to lay out for them a full statement of the principles of the gospel he preached. In the book of Romans, Paul clearly lays out the plan of salvation through the grace of God, and not by the works of man. The overall theme of the book of Romans is *The Righteousness of God in the Gospel of Christ.* We are justified by faith in God because of the free gift of salvation bought and paid for by the shed blood of Jesus our Lord. Major teaching in the book of Romans includes:

- All have sinned.
- Justification is by faith alone.
- Practicing righteousness in the Christian life.
- God and Israel.
- Practical applications.
- Paul's ministry and plans.

First Corinthians is a pastoral letter, written to resolve doctrinal and practical problems within the local church. Paul had established the church at Corinth about 50-51 AD, when he spent eighteen months there on his second missionary journey. (See Acts 18:1-17.)

Second Corinthians consists of three main parts. The first seven chapters contain Paul's defense of his conduct and his ministry. The second part, chapters 8 and 9, deal with the offering being raised by Paul for the poor saints in Judea. Chapters 10 through 13 contain a message of rebuke to certain parties in the church. Here are the major teachings of 1 and 2 Corinthians:

- Paul addresses sectarianism within the church.
- Paul addresses several problems in the church including: church discipline, lawsuits between Christians, sexual misuse of the body, relationship problems concerning sex, marriage, and slavery, ethical problems concerning eating food offered to idols, the problem of desecrating the Lord's supper, and problems which arose from the misuse of the spiritual gifts.
- Generosity in giving.
- Defense and use of apostolic authority.

Galatians is the only letter Paul specifically addressed to a group of churches. Galatia wasn't a city, but a region of Asia Minor which included many towns. Many of the Jews in Galatia, though not denying that faith in Jesus was necessary, still maintained that you must also follow the Law. Once again, in the book of Galatians, Paul has to proclaim the doctrine of justification by faith alone. Here's the major teaching in the book of Galatians:

- Paul denounces the Judaizers.
- Paul defends his apostolic authority.
- Paul defends the gospel.
- Paul exhorts the Galatians to properly use their Christian liberty, to walk in the Spirit, and bear one another's burdens.
- Warning against the legalists.

While Paul was imprisoned in Rome, he wrote to the **Ephesians**. Ephesus was a principal port on the west coast of Asia Minor. The church at Ephesus is also one of the churches Jesus addressed in the book of the Revelation. Paul's letter to the Ephesians reveals the "mystery" of the church. The word "glory" appears eight times and refers to the exceeding excellence of God's love, His wisdom, and His power. Paul talks about Jesus' goal to build a glorious church, "not having spot or wrinkle." Here's some of the teaching you'll find in Paul's letter to the Ephesians:

- The believer's position in Christ.
- The believer's past, present, and future.
- The apostle's prayer for power.
- The believer's call to responsibility.
- The believer's call to purity.
- The believer's call to Spirit-filled living.

It's believed that Paul wrote his letter to the **Philippians** during his first Roman imprisonment, about AD 61. Paul had established this church at Philippi during his second missionary journey, about AD 51. The biggest message of the book of Philippians is joy in Christ. The joy Paul was speaking of is joy that comes from our relationship *with* Christ. In Philippians 4:4, Paul says, ***"Rejoice in the Lord always. Again I will say, rejoice!"*** In Paul's letter to the Philippians you'll find:

- Circumstances of Paul's imprisonment.
- Several exhortations such as: live worthy of the gospel; reproduce the mind of Christ; cultivate the spiritual life.
- Warnings against error.

Paul had never visited Colosse, which was a small town in the province of Asia, 100 miles east of Ephesus. It's possible that the church at Colosse met in Philemon's home. (See Philemon 2.) Paul had to write to the **Colossians** to counteract false teachers at Colosse who had undermined many major doctrines of Christianity — one of which was the deity of Christ. No other book in the New Testament more fully defends the universal lordship of Jesus. Here's what you'll see in the letter to the Colossians:

- Paul's prayer of praise for their faith, and prayer for their growth in Christ.
- Christ's supremacy displayed.
- Christ's supremacy and sufficiency defended.
- Christ's supremacy demanded in Christian living.

First and **Second Thessalonians** were also written by Paul. During Paul's short term ministry in Athens, Paul became concerned with the newly begun church at Thessalonica. In 1 Thessalonians, you see relief and thankfulness that the church is growing. Paul also discusses brotherly love, marital fidelity, and the second coming of Christ. Paul's second letter to the Thessalonians is similar to the first. The return of the Lord is the central part of both letters.

First and **Second Timothy** were also written by — that's right — *Paul*. The primary purpose of these letters was to encourage Timothy in his rather difficult assignment of dealing with doctrinal errors and practical problems in the church at Ephesus. In Paul's second letter to Timothy, he urges Timothy to be faithful in the face of hardships. These two letters, plus Titus, make up what are called the Pastoral Epistles. Here's what you'll find in 1 and 2 Timothy:

- Instructions concerning the church.
- Instructions concerning pastoral duties.
- Faithfulness in the face of hardship, desertions, and error.

Titus was evidently a Greek who was converted by Paul. Titus, who was a young preacher of the gospel, was assigned to work in Crete. Paul wrote to Titus to give him instructions concerning the performance of his pastoral duties. The letter to Titus contains:

- Instructions concerning elders.
- Instructions concerning Christian conduct.
- Instructions concerning teaching spiritual truths, and avoiding dissension.

Paul's letter to **Philemon**, who was a wealthy Christian slave owner, was a personal appeal for a slave named Onesimus. Apparently, Onesimus had run away to Rome after stealing his master's property. In Rome, Paul led Onesimus to Christ. Paul's ultimate goal was to see Philemon receive Onesimus as a brother in Christ. This letter shows the wonderful love of Christ and how He can bring love and forgiveness into broken lives.

Hebrews does not name its author. This letter was written to Jewish believers who were faltering in their faith. The climax of the this letter is the presentation of the high priestly of ministry of Jesus. Chapter 11 lists some of the great heroes of faith from the Old Testament. Chapter 11 has come to be known the "Hall of Faith." Here's some of the major teaching in the letter to the Hebrews:

- The superiority of Jesus.
- The superiority of Jesus' ministry.
- Jesus has provided a better covenant.
- A call to full assurance of faith.
- The heroes of the faith.
- Admonition to love.

The author of the next letter simply identifies himself as **James**. The New Testament lists at least five men named James. Two of them were Jesus' disciples, and one was His brother. Tradition ascribes this book to James the brother of Jesus who became the leader of the church at Jerusalem. The book of James is mainly a practical and ethical teaching, emphasizing being a "doer of the Word." Here is the teaching you'll encounter in the book of James:

- Practical religion and trials.
- Hear the Word, receive the Word, obey the Word.
- Practical Christianity concerning speech, worldliness, and business.

First and **Second Peter** were written by — man you're getting good! Peter's first letter speaks to Christians living in parts of Asia Minor who are suffering rejection in the world because of their obedience to Christ. However, Peter's second letter warns Christians against false teachers within their own fellowship who could lead them into apostasy (falling away). First and Second Peter contain:

- Rejoicing in the hope of Christ's return.
- Righteous living in everyday circumstances.
- Suffering for Christ's sake.

- True versus false teaching.
- Description and destruction of false teachers.
- Scoffers in the last days.

First, Second, and **Third John** were written by the apostle John. First John stresses the themes of love, light, knowledge, and life in its warnings against heresy. Second John (only 13 verses long) encourages "the elect lady" to continue showing hospitality, and stresses that *truth* be the basis for Christian fellowship. The third letter provides a picture of the church as a family bound together by love and hospitality toward one another.

Jude identifies himself as the "brother of James." Jude is very purposeful in his warning against an unidentified group of false teachers. Jude says, "These are sensual (worldly) persons, who cause divisions, not having the Spirit." They obviously had a big problem with false teachers in the beginning stages of the church. The book of Jude ends on a positive note, giving glory to God — *"To God our Savior, who alone is wise, be glory and majesty, dominion and power, both now and forever, Amen."*

The Revelation of Jesus Christ is, appropriately, the last book in the New Testament. Early church tradition unanimously attributes this book to the apostle John. The central message of the book of The Revelation is not the beast and the great tribulation. The book of *The Revelation of Jesus Christ* is centered on the message that ***"the Lord God Omnipotent reigns!"*** *(Revelations 19:6).*

John received these prophecies through a series of visions he received concerning the great tribulation, the judgment, and heaven and hell. The events in the book of

The Revelation *are not* in chronological order. There are two stories that unfold: one is the story of events in heaven, and the other is the story of events happening on earth. Interwoven are chapters containing information about these two stories. Here is some of what you'll find in the book of The Revelation:

- The letters to the seven churches.
- The seven seals, the seven trumpets, the seven signs, the seven bowls.
- The supper of the great God.
- The war and Satan bound.
- Living and reigning with Christ.
- Satan released to deceive.
- The Great White Throne Judgment.
- The new heaven and the new earth.
- The New Jerusalem.
- The bride of the Lamb.
- Final warning and assurance.

Bible Interpretation

Now let's examine a few basic rules of Bible interpretation. Generally speaking, if you stick with these rules, you can avoid error in interpreting the Bible.

1. Scripture interprets scripture.

In other words, God doesn't say one thing in the Old Testament and something different in the New Testament. I can hear the screaming and shouting now. Some are saying, "There are many things in the Old Testament that are different than the New!"

You're right! For instance, in the Old Testament many men were allowed to have multiple wives, and in the New Testament it tells us we must be the husband of one wife.

So, in light of Bible interpretation we must ask ourselves, was it *God's will* that men have multiple wives in the Old Testament, or was it *man's choice*?

Remember the saying, "In the Old the New is contained, and in the New the Old is explained." *As a general rule*, we do not interpret New Testament teaching by the Old Testament. You cannot force New Testament standards of morality on Old Testament passages because the Old Testament is *incomplete in it's revelation of God.* God is not double-minded. Hebrews 13:8 says, *"Jesus Christ is the same yesterday, today, and forever."* Keep that in mind as you interpret scripture. **There are five contexts** we must consider when interpreting passages:

a. *The context of the passage* — i.e. What do the verses before and after say? If a passage of the scripture you're reading is dealing with family relationships, don't pull one scripture out to try to prove a point about the second coming of Christ. Keep the verse in its proper setting.

b. *Context of the entire book* — i.e. In the book of Romans, Paul talks about justification by faith.

c. *Other books by the same author* — i.e. Solomon wrote most of the book of Proverbs, Ecclesiastes, and the Song of Solomon. What was Solomon like? What was the main thrust of his other books?

d. *The entire Testament (Old or New)* — i.e. In the Old Testament we see more of the judgment side of God, while in the New Testament we see more of the grace and mercy side of God.

e. *The entire Bible.* As I've already said, God is not double-minded. We need to interpret His Words *(ultimately)* in light of the Bible as a whole.

2. The Bible is a progressive revelation.

This means that it's the successive unfolding of a continuous theme to its consummation. *Which means*, God has revealed Himself a little at a time. We must view the entire picture in order to get a proper revelation of who God is. If you just read the Old Testament by itself, you might come to the conclusion that God is very harsh and judgmental. But when you see God further revealed in the New Testament, you gain a better understanding of His unparalleled love toward mankind.

3. The Bible is to be interpreted literally.

This, of course, is done in light of the writers style, grammar, and setting. The Bible contains three different styles of literature:

a. *Prose*: Includes all history and teaching.
b. *Poetry*: Includes one-third of the Old Testament.
c. *Apocalyptic*: Prophetic; meaning is hidden in symbolism.

Also, there's a difference between interpretation and application. As a general rule, there is only one truth to a passage. However, there may be several *applications*. i.e. "Don't give place to the devil" — there is one specific truth, but several applications.

4. **The Bible must be interpreted in light of history and culture.**

By history we mean: date, author, and environment. i.e. First Corinthians 11:10, Paul talks about women's head coverings. In the middle- eastern culture today, women are still required to cover their heads in public. But in our culture, they are not.

In some cultures, as in Jesus' day, it's OK for Christians to drink wine or small amounts of alcohol. But, because of the abuse and the stigma attached to alcohol in our culture, it's not acceptable for Christians to drink alcohol. What would you think if you saw your pastor going in the corner liquor store and coming out with a bottle? *That's what I thought.*

5. **Interpret the Bible in light of who is doing the talking, and whom they're talking to.**

Determine who is talking, whom they're talking to, *and what is the subject matter*. There are some instances where Jesus was talking only to the nation of Israel. There are some prophecies in the Old Testament that were "conditional" prophecies for Israel at that particular time and place in history.

Those are a few basic rules of Bible interpretation. Now, let's put it into practice. Let me give you an example of a passage that I believe could be interpreted *differently* in light of these rules. I've chosen this particular passage because ultimately its interpretation has very little significance or bearing on our larger more important doctrinal beliefs. So in other words, whether you agree or disagree — *Who really cares!* But, it may help you remember and put into practice, these rules of Bible interpretation.

In Genesis 3:1 it says, *"Now the serpent was more cunning than any beast of the field which the Lord had made. And he said to the woman, "Has God indeed said, "You shall not eat of every tree of the garden?"* Well, you know the rest of the story. I don't know about you, but since I was a child I was taught that a *serpent* **literally** came up and began speaking to Eve.

Now, what's the first rule? **Scripture interprets scripture.** Question: Where else in the Bible do we see *the devil* make an animal talk? Don't say Balaam's donkey! *God* made Balaam's donkey talk. We do see the devil *referred to* as a roaring lion and a dragon. In 1 Peter 5:8, it tells us that the devil is *like* a roaring lion, and in Revelation 20:2 it says, *"He laid hold of the dragon, that serpent of old, who is the devil...."* It seems pretty obvious that the names ascribed to the devil are metaphors used to describe his deceitful, devilish attributes.

The context of the book — Question: Where else in creation (in the garden) do we see any animal talk? If no other animal in creation talked, don't you think Eve would have been a little freaked out by a snake coming up and having a conversation with her? If God created animals to talk in the original creation, He would have given them the ability to think like humans (mind, will, and emotions), and they would have had the equipment to be able to talk. (voice box, etc.) In that case, man *would not* have been created *above*, or superior to, the animals. Hmmm...

What about **grammar, style, and setting/custom and culture?** *If* Moses authored the book of Genesis (many believe he did), consider the problem he had with fiery serpents. In Numbers 21:7 the Lord sent fiery serpents among the people, they bit the people, and many of the people of Israel died. Not to mention, Moses had grown up in Egypt and the Egyptians worshipped all kinds of animals including the serpent. It's possible that Moses used the serpent *to represent the devil* in Genesis because of the devil's obvious snake-like attributes.

We know who's doing the talking and who they're talking to. But, what about when God tells the devil in Genesis 3:14, *"on your belly you shall go, and you shall eat dust all the days of your life."* Let me say this, if you have several pieces of evidence pointing in one direction, don't give up your investigation because of *one* piece that seems to contradict. Of course, the opposite is true as well. **Don't** make a doctrine out of *one piece of scripture* when you have *several* that point another direction.

If Moses is using the term "serpent" as a metaphor in Genesis 3:1, then why wouldn't he continue to do so in Genesis 3:14? Have you ever heard a really angry person say to another angry person, "Man, I'm gonna make you crawl and eat dirt" (or something like that)? Could it be that Moses was simply describing an expression of extreme humiliation and defeat concerning the devil? Could it be that the devil deceived Eve the same way he tries to deceive us today?

Well, that's enough to contemplate for now. I hope you have enjoyed the lesson on Bible interpretation. Tune in any time. I hope reading this book has not only helped bring life a little more into focus from a biblical perspective, but also sparked within you a sense of destiny *and* victory.

Most of all, I pray that you have a renewed, *or stronger* passion for God and His Word. The Bible is *not* just a textbook. **The Bible is life!** Don't be overwhelmed by it! Get to know it! I can hear it calling you right now. *You better go find out what He wants.*

About the Author

Jeff Canfield served six years in the Army National Guard and eight years in municipal law enforcement. Jeff is a graduate of Rhema Bible Training Center in Broken Arrow, Oklahoma. Currently, Jeff pastors a church in Sullivan, Indiana, where he resides with his wife Lori, and their two children, Courtney and Nathan.